From Mathura to Manorama

feminist fine print is a moderately priced, handy new series that offers two, three or four core essays on a single issue, from a critical feminist perspective. The essays may be single-authored or have multiple authorship, depending on the issue, its significance within India and South Asia, and its theoretical and political implications.

feminist fine print

From Mathura to Manorama

Resisting Violence Against Women in India

Kalpana Kannabiran &
Ritu Menon

women UNLIMITED
an associate of
kali for women

International Centre
for Ethnic Studies

From Mathura to Manorama:
Resisting Violence Against Women in India
was first published in 2007 by

Women Unlimited
(an associate of Kali for Women)
K–36, Hauz Khas Enclave, Ground Floor,
New Delhi 110 016

ISBN: 81-88965-35-9

Cover design: peali@pealistudio.com

This research and publication are an outcome of a research project undertaken by the International Centre for Ethnic Studies, Colombo. Research for the project was financially supported by the Canadian International Development Agency's South Asia Regional Gender Project. The views and opinions expressed in this book do not in any way represent the views of CIDA or the South Asia Regional Gender Project.

Typeset at Tulika Print Comunication Services,
35A/1 Shahpur Jat, New Delhi 110 049, and printed at
Pauls Press, E 44/11 Okhla Phase II, New Delhi 110 020

Contents

Acknowledgements

We are grateful to A.K. Visalakshi, student at the National University of Juridical Sciences, Calcutta, P. Supriya Rao, student at the Delhi School of Social Work, Sowmya Kumar and Ruchira Kulkarni, students at NALSAR University of Law, and Sana Aiyer and Bhashwati Sengupta for research support; Seema Sagar of Women Unlimited and P. Sujatha, V.U.V.S. Subbalakshmi and V. Padmini from Asmita for secretarial assistance; Faiz Ahmed of Women Unlimited and K. Sarah and R. Sudha from Asmita for assistance in financial administration.

We are also grateful to Nimanthi Rajasingham of the International Centre for Ethnic Studies (Colombo) for her inputs, assistance and unfailing support during the project period; and to Radhika Coomaraswamy and members of the ICES project from Sri Lanka and Pakistan for comments and feedback on early drafts of the manuscript.

KALPANA KANNABIRAN
RITU MENON

New Delhi, Hyderabad
November 2006

1 From Mathura to Manorama

Kalpana Kannabiran &

Ritu Menon

- *IN 1980, a teenage Muslim girl was gang-raped by three policemen and the son of a bootlegger in a village near Bombay. After a great deal of mobilization by the Forum Against Rape (a women's organization in the city), in the form of area meetings, street theatre, songs and slogan campaigns, as well as protest marches in front of the police station, this was the outcome: arrest warrants were issued against 11 women who were charged with hooliganism, trespassing on the police station and beating up the police!*[1]

- *NP, a lesbian woman, wrote to Counsel Club, the Calcutta-based organization working on issues of gay, lesbian, bisexual and transgendered people, about the murder of her lesbian partner, Mou, by her husband. "Just a month back, Mou was stabbed to death by some miscreant hired by my husband. He had come to know everything. He could not cause any harm to me because of a fear of public scandal.... That fateful night that Mou was killed...my husband raped me.... At the time of putting force on me for sexual intercourse, my husband depicted to me how Mou was killed."*[2]

- *As the sun was setting on March 11, 2002, in Chargaon village of Chitrakoot, 20-year old Ragini (name changed), a Dalit woman, set off to the fields to answer the call of nature. On the way, Raju Upadhyay of the same village raped her in the fields. Ragini reported the matter to her in-laws with whom she lived. As they were leaving to file an FIR, some influential men from the village stopped them and asked them to settle the issue in the Panchayat. Ex-*

cept for two, all the members of the Panchayat were Brahmin men. For the next seven days the survivor and her family were pressurized not to make an issue of the rape. Finally Ragini met the Karvi legislator, R.K. Patel, and the Superintendent of Police. After their telephonic instructions the local police station lodged her FIR. On March 20, Dr Nidhi at the Mau P.H.C medically examined her, and after another two days the culprit was arrested on March 22, 2002. In July 2002 Ragini received Rs. 25,000 from the Social Welfare Department for, according to her father-in-law, expenses towards fighting her case. Six months later the culprit was released on bail and is roaming around scot-free, threatening the survivor and her family with dire consequences.[3]

- *On July 11, 2004, at 3:30 pm, Havildar Suresh Kumar in Imphal (Manipur) signed a memo stating that he was arresting Thangjam Manorama Devi, 32 years old, "a suspected insurgent, explosives expert and hardcore member" of the banned People's Liberation Army (PLA). Three hours later she was found dead, having been raped and shot in her vagina. On July 15, four days after Manorama was killed, the entire country was stunned to see photographs in the national press of a most extraordinary protest—15 middle-aged women demonstrated naked in front of the gates of Kangla Fort, HQ of the 17 Assam Rifles, shouting, "Indian Army, Rape Us!" Said 75-year-old Thockchom Ramani, secretary of the Women's Social Reformation and Development Samaj, "Our anger made us shed us our inhibitions that day. If necessary, we will die, commit self-immolation to save our innocent sons and daughters."*[4]

I

Central to the women's movement, worldwide, has been the issue of rape, around which have cohered consciousness-raising, analysis and activism in the form of demonstrations, protests, campaigning and lobbying for legal reform. As women and feminists began to examine the physical, social, emotional, criminal and gender dimensions of this extreme violation of women's bodies, an outline of its full import began to emerge. Susan Brownmiller's classic text on it, *Against Our Will: Men, Women and Rape* remains a benchmark analysis; but as the complex and specific character of the crime unfolded, more sophisticated—and debatable—positions gained ground. Radical feminists proposed that the very physical difference between men and women made rape a uniquely male act—men rape women because they can. The sexual domination of women by men forms the crux of this argument: rape, or the threat of rape, keeps most women subjugated by, in fear of, and under the control of men. Liberal feminists differed with this almost biological explanation and saw rape as a crime made possible by social sanction, male power and privilege, and unequal gender relations. They believed in, and campaigned for, legal change, placing their trust in an effective legal system that would deliver justice to women victims of rape once the legal hurdles had been crossed. Marxist feminists, on the other hand, located rape and other forms of violence against women in a material and economic context, adding an analysis of class relations to our understanding of the oppression of women. Finally, socialist feminists proposed that only a comprehensive review of class, patriarchy and structural and systemic violence could provide an adequate explanation for the whole range of violations that women are subjected to; in other words, they emphasized the links between violence and the economic exploitation of women; violence and sexuality; reproductive labour and male violence; and more recently, between race, class and gender; or caste, class and gender—and violence.[5]

In the twenty-odd years between the 1980 protest by Forum Against Rape and the demonstration by Manipuri women in Imphal in 2004, feminist activists and academics in India have not only had to deal with spiralling violence against women and the ramified forms in which it presents itself, but also with seriously reviewing their own strategies and mobilization on it. Within the movement itself, there is no single, common thread that binds it together, nor an agreed theoretical analysis or political position. Left-oriented women outside political parties may come together with party-affiliated groups on specific issues, but will part company with them on analysis or strategy. Similarly, more radical or lesbian feminists may, by and large, agree with other women's groups on strategy, but not on analysis or conceptualization. Notwithstanding this, however, a minimum consensus has evolved over the past three decades in the autonomous women's movement, that rejects any rationalisation of violence against women and recognizes the complexity of fields of violence—sometimes familial, sometimes heterosexual, sometimes homophobic, sometimes communal, sometimes casteist, now individual, now collective but seen together—as cumulative and intersectional tools of patriarchal power. These complex, interlocking fields of violence have resulted in extremely significant shifts in the methods and fields of organizing within women's movements, and a critical expansion of their scope, as women's groups (*a*) ally with other social movements working on issues of social and economic justice; and (*b*) see a growing number of working/toiling women asserting their rights in association with them. As Omvedt says, "They are doing so in a context of growing social violence, economic polarisation, political degeneration and ecological destruction, with the tide of religious fundamentalism threatening a reasserted patriarchy."[6]

Simultaneously, the movement has been called upon to address a whole array of forms of violence that have surfaced in the years since Mathura and Rameeza Bi—revenge gang-rape; power rape; the rape of lower caste women by upper caste men; "honour" killings; ethnic and communal sexual violence; the slow spread of dowry killings across the country; violence against women in situations of armed conflict; economic violence; the pre-birth elimination of female foetuses; sexual violence by the state; and so on. This has enabled it to arrive at some insights and conceptual breakthroughs which we will elaborate later, following a brief description of how the terrain has changed over the last quarter century of mobilizing and resisting.

II

Early national campaigns on violence against women focused on dowry murders and custodial rape, bringing both to sustained public attention through a combination of strategies: media exposure; public interest litigation; demonstrations and protests; and intense lobbying for changes in the law. Gandhi and Shah characterize this as the "process of politicization"; the collective use of forms of political protest like street demonstrations, anti-state slogans and dharnas, they say, transformed these "social" issues into political ones, the "private" into public, thus holding state and society responsible for atrocities on women.[7] At a mass level, they continue, consciousness-raising took place through poster exhibitions, street plays, songs and audio-visual shows.[8]

Each of these strategies has had a greater or lesser degree of success, and all have come in for serious reconsideration by analysts and activists over the two decades under review. As far as legislation is concerned, the Dowry Prohibition (Amendment) Act, 1984 may be considered a landmark and a major victory for the movement. Not merely a victory, however: it was also considered to be a vindication of a particular form of mobilizing, awareness-building and strategizing—in other words, ends and means were mutually reinforcing.

Similarly, the addition of several new sections to the Indian Penal Code (IPC), the Code of Criminal Procedure (CrPC) and the Indian Evidence Act (IEA) made significant advances on earlier provisions regarding rape in these laws, by recognizing the importance of withholding the victim's name in published reports; redefining consent; criminalizing custodial rape; recognizing that forcible intercourse with a separated wife is considered rape. With respect to evidence the most important shifts have been the inversion of the "innocent until proved guilty" principle that is the cornerstone of criminal justice in rape trials. A new section, 114 A, was written into the Evidence Act according to which, if a woman stated that she did not consent to sexual intercourse, the court would presume in her favour and the accused would have to prove that he was not guilty of assault. Moreover, by the early 1980s, the difficult issue of corroboration was settled in favour of the woman-victim; her version could be relied upon without corroboration.[9] Also significant is the fact that, for the first time, minimum punishment for rape was specified in Section 376 IPC: ten years rigorous imprisonment for custodial rape, gang-rape, the rape of pregnant women, and girls below 12 years of age; and seven years for all other kinds of rape. The meaning of "custody" under Section 376 (2) (a)(b)&(c) included as custodians, police officers, public servants, the management and staff of hospitals, jails, remand homes and institutions for women and children. The maximum term for any of these offences could extend to imprisonment for life. At the time, two major lacunae in legislation were identified: a failure to incorporate marital rape into the amendments; and to frame a comprehensive law on domestic violence as a whole. A review meeting held by women's groups in the early 1990s, in Bombay, to evaluate the effectiveness of the rape and dowry legislations came up with yet another important anomaly: the absence in existing law of any distinction between the rape of minors and infants, and that of adults. This anomaly persists to this day, despite comprehensive draft legislation on rape being presented by expert groups and the Law Commission's own recommendations on reform, made in its 172nd Report of 2000.[10]

The review meeting referred to above took into

account the roughly ten years of prosecution, arrests and conviction made by the state under both the Dowry Prohibition Act and the new amendments in the rape law. At a fundamental level, the consensus was that both pieces of legislation have been regrettably inadequate, indeed largely ineffective; one major reason for this is the misogyny and suspicion which pervade all legislation on crimes against women, and which find an echo in courtrooms. According to feminist lawyer, Flavia Agnes, "Procedures continued to be long and harrowing, the investigative machinery lax and corrupt, cross-examinations of the victims degrading and humiliating and, contrary to expectations, the statistics revealed an increase in reported cases and a dismal rate of conviction."[11]

On dowry murders, too, the experience of seeking justice through the police and courts has been extremely negative, despite the introduction of several amendments to the CrPC, specifically Section 498A, which pertains to dowry-related harassment and violence. Procedural and legal recalcitrance apart, women's groups, feminist lawyers, activists and academics were forced to admit that changes in law alone were an insufficient guarantee of justice; and more critically, that social and familial pressures, cultural biases against divorced or separated women, and women's own economic dependence on abusive relationships within marriage were responsible for the persistence of dowry murders. As with rape, which ramified into an alarming range of violations mentioned earlier, so too, "bride-burning" or "dowry deaths" spiralled into detailed explorations of domestic violence, and the extremely disadvantageous position of women vis-à-vis rights in inheritance in both natal and marital homes.[12] The most vicious and murderous manifestation of this is the pre-birth elimination of female foetuses, a practice that has grown alarmingly in the last decade, with disastrous consequences on the sex ratio across the country. The inability of the law, and of state and central legislation, to curb sex selection and female foeticide is glaringly evident.

Why then, has every campaign in the movement, especially one dealing with violence against women, demanded legal reform? Despite our severe criticism of the legal system and our recognition of its intrinsic patriarchalism, why do we persist in seeking newer and more far-reaching legislation? When justice is so elusive as to appear unattainable, why do we still encourage women to report the crimes committed against them and replay the violence done to them? Upendra Baxi, noted jurist and legal theorist, sees a transition between four sets of attitudes in the women's movement:

> The 'nihilists' . . . suspect that all law talk is a ruse to divert and deflect, and to depoliticise the nature and agenda of the struggle for women's emancipation. 'Evangelists' show, in deep contrast, an abiding commitment to the rule of law… The 'moderates' appreciate the potential role of law but believe that legal changes in themselves are not likely to usher significant social changes. . . The 'eclectics' will use it without thinking much about the significance of the use of the law for social thought and action.[13]

In their defence, even the most optimistic among the liberals in the movement do not believe that laws alone can change social discrimination and customs, or that the state is an impartial dispenser of justice. On the contrary, as Gandhi and Shah maintain, "the majority of women's groups see legal reform as a broad strategy for challenging the inferior position of women; for legitimacy and social recognition of their issues; and for some short term legal redress."[14] Moreover, legal campaigning as a strategy has emerged as part of the political practice of the movement; by moving "personal" issues such as domestic violence and dowry deaths into the legal domain it has redefined the concept of women's rights. In one sense, the women's movement has even occasionally subverted the law by dispensing an "alternative" justice, and exposing the frailties and biases of the legal system against women in the process. The efforts by Muslim women in Pudukottai in Tamil Nadu to build a women's mosque is a case in point. Finding both the formal and customary courts weighted against them, women got together to constitute the Muslim women's jamaat, which then began to hear cases of domestic violence and provide immediate relief and redress to victims. While the idea was resisted initially, in a short period of time the local community conceded that justice was, in fact, being done better than before.[15]

Actual work on the ground by women's groups on rape and dowry murders, including legal aid, counselling and providing shelter, led to a closer examination of the nature of violence against women. Dowry deaths, for instance, came to be seen as only the tip of the iceberg, with a whole array of domestic abuse, battery and physical and psychological violence underlying that dramatic and extraordinary manifestation of it. The protracted, pervasive, everyday violence against women and children in the domestic space opened up a distressing new vista, calling for the kind of action and analysis that seemed inadequate to the enormity of the problem.

Detailed micro studies by individual scholars, the International Center for Research on Women, as well as national level findings by the National Family Health Survey (First & Second Rounds), the Muslim Women's Survey and the National Sample Survey Organisation, and Sahayatrika, a lesbian women's collective in Kerala, established the extent and spread of violence by age, class, caste, community, location and sexual orientation; they also correlated the incidence and type of violence experienced—mental, physical, verbal, psychological, sporadic, regular, and so on—by respondents' level of education, employment, and marital status.[16] One alarming finding common to all studies is the acceptance of violence by women, and the extent to which their subservience and subordination have been internalised: close to 50 per cent of the women surveyed by the NFHS were of the view that they "deserved" the violence meted out to them. Comprehensive legislation on this was proposed by a collective of women's organizations, coordinated by the Lawyers' Collective, but this time the emphasis was on a combination of criminal and civil remedies. Domestic violence was not made synonymous with inter-spousal violence, and for the first time, the domestic relationship was expanded to include unmarried daughters, widows, sisters, mothers-in-law and dependents; equally significantly, any relationship "in the nature of marriage" also came within the purview of the bill. A woman's rights to residence, to maintenance, and to custody of her children were guaranteed through the provision of protection orders on all three, violation of which would be treated as a criminal offence. The Bill was passed in 2005.

III

Feminist campaigns on the issue of violence against women were tied closely to the development of legal principles and the crafting of a jurisprudence equipped to deal with the issues that women's groups consistently brought before the courts. The human rights campaign against custodial violence during the 1975 Emergency, that gained ground in the late 1970s and early '80s, was particularly significant for the women's movement, because sexual assault against women in custody was a critical issue. The cases that brought this issue to the centre of human rights campaigns were those of Mathura in Maharashtra and Rameeza Bi in Andhra Pradesh. Both raised a range of questions that continue to be relevant today. The most significant of these had to do with the reinforcement of patriarchal norms by the criminal justice system, through a discourse that locked women into intersecting cycles of violence. Feminists and human rights activists realised with a shock that what seemed to determine whether a woman had been raped was not the "objective" assessment of evidence before the court, but her past sexual history. In the proceedings of the Justice Muktadar Commission of Inquiry to investigate the rape of Rameeza Bi and the death of Ahmed Hussain in police custody, the defendent police officers did not attempt to prove that there had been no rape, but to cast aspersions on her character. There was a procession of witnesses who testified that Rameeza had been married countless times; that her marriage to Ahmed Hussain was not a valid Muslim marriage; and that, in fact, she was a prostitute who had been caught by the police while she was soliciting.[17] With Mathura as well, the judgement spoke of her immorality and low character, leading to the historic Open Letter to the Supreme Court by Vasudha Dhagamwar, Upendra Baxi and Lotika Sarkar.[18] The consequent demand by women's groups that past sexual history cannot determine or influence the outcome of rape trials has since become a firm legal principle that is adhered to at least rhetorically, forcing judges to re-examine the bases of their own biases and discomfort about bringing justice to women.

However, it is important to remember that although the question of past sexual history has been interrogated at the level of appellate courts and in law reform endeavours, the category of the "habituated woman," the "two-finger test," and the medico-theoretical possibility of inflicting injuries on oneself in order to press false charges, were left completely untouched by feminist campaigns.[19] While there was a nuancing of the notion of consent in penal law, the medicalisation of consent in medical jurisprudence retained anatomical codes that were deeply patriarchal.

At around the same time there was an outburst of another kind of horrific violence against women. Kerosene stoves across the country started exploding in what seemed like an epidemic, claiming the lives of newly married women by engulfing them in flames. Or, in a variation, these very young women suddenly began to find it impossible to cope with "stomach pain" and were committing suicide en masse. The state distanced itself from the scene. The issue did not figure for civil liberties groups because the state was not a "perpetrator". The task of investigating individual cases and pursuing them in courts, as well as of campaigning for women's right to life within the family, was left entirely to women's groups. It was in this context that the slogan, "the personal is the political" began to be applied for the first time. Consciousness-raising included raising the consciousness of human rights activists on the connections between the private and the public, and pointing to the fallacy of this distinction when it concerned domestic violence. The continuities between rape and death in custody on the one hand, and practices of domestic violence and the murder of wives on the other; the transformation of "private violence" into a human rights issue; the shared immunity between state actors and non-state dominant actors; the resolution of the "morality-immorality" fix where women survivors were concerned; the baffling situation of the impossibility of full redress against any form of violence that women are subjected to; the ways in which patriarchy and violence coalesce, conflating women's experiences in private and public spaces and erasing the difference between sexual harassment and sexual assault, are issues that are understood in all their complexity today because of concerted campaigns by women's groups across the country.

A closer review of the kinds of changes incorporated in laws as a consequence of campaigning by the women's movement is available in Ch. 2, but a brief recapitulation of the major founding campaigns of the resistance to violence against women may be in order here. At the 1991 meeting in Bombay, for instance, recommendations on the rape law made by women's groups may be summarised as follows: child sexual abuse, largely neglected by law, was sought to be brought within the definition of sexual assault; it was argued that penetration, hitherto confined to penile-vaginal penetration resulting in acquittal or mitigation of sentences, must be redefined to mean penetration whether anal, with objects, or any other method in order to encompass the range of assaults women and children are subjected to; women's consent should be defined to mean "unequivocal voluntary agreement". The entire effort was aimed at bringing boys under the age of sixteen, and women of all ages within the ambit of a comprehensive law on sexual assault. While the Law Commission agreed with most suggestions made by women's groups, the two matters on which it demurred were the definition of consent—which the Commission felt had already been adequately defined and established through case law—and removing the exception to Section 375, thereby bringing marital rape within the ambit of rape. This, the Law Commission felt, would constitute unnecessary interference in the institution of marriage.

The procedural aspects of rape law are, in fact, as crucial as its penal aspects. Delineating the former in fair detail, the draft by the Law Commission incorporated the experience of women's groups when dealing with cases of sexual assault on the ground. On granting bail to a person accused of sexual assault, for instance, it recommended that one of the conditions imposed by the court be that such a person not be in proximity to the person assaulted. Nor should the criminal justice process, in any manner whatsoever, interfere with or disturb the natural habitat of the person assaulted. It called for a limitation of time, six months, for the investigation and trial of sexual offences. It also proposed that the expression 'social worker' should mean *a woman* interested in, or working for, the cause of women and/or children, who is familiar with issues of violence against women and children.

With respect to Evidence Law, one problem that has confounded rape cases has been the question of consent. While the Law Commission felt it was not necessary to define consent in the new legislation it proposed that,

> [a] new section . . . should be introduced in the Evidence Act stating that wherein a prosecution for aggravated sexual assault under Sections 376A to 376D of the IPC, the question is whether the person so assaulted consented to it and where such person states before the court that he/she did not so consent, the court shall presume it to be so.

Further, it recommended that two sections in the Evidence Act (146 and 155), which refer to past sexual history, be deleted. It may be recalled that these sections first came into question in the Mathura and Rameeza Bi cases, where such sexual history was used not to disprove the assault, but to exonerate the accused. These provisions in the law were first problematised by feminist groups and subjected to a larger critique of the patriarchal basis of criminal law, especially that dealing with sexual assault on women—whether "outraging modesty" or rape. Further, in view of the fact that the accusation of rape relied heavily on medical and forensic reports, and that it was physically impossible for assaulted women and children to ensure medical examination in the stipulated time, the recommendation to the Law Commission drew on the experiences of women, by stating that the "absence of a medical report in the case of a sexual assault shall not be a factor against the complainant/person assaulted". While providing additional safeguards against further trauma in the case of children who have been subjected to abuse, the recommendations urge that all officers in every part of the criminal justice system relating to cases of sexual assault, be trained and sensitized in dealing with them. After decades of finding that patriarchal predisposition and biases hinder a basic understanding of women's experience of sexual assault, there is an urgent need for judicial and other officers who empathise with women's discrimination under patriarchy. While judges acknowledge that a greater number of women in the judiciary will make a difference to the judicial view of women's experience, especially of sexual assault, representation continues to be a silent issue, particularly in high courts and the Supreme Court. Even the Law Commission Report only speaks of greater sensitivity and understanding, not greater representation.

It is pertinent at this point to reflect on the continuum of violence that women's groups have had to campaign against over a period of three decades. While earlier cases had to do with custodial violence—rape, to be more specific—the framework for locating this crime was fairly clear since it came within the ambit of state violence in the civil liberties paradigm. Questions of identity, dominance, location, while mentioned in passing, were not material to the analysis of their predicament, in relation to the majoritarian state or the criminal justice system. Yet, interestingly, the first two major cases of custodial rape that became symbols of the women's movement in India, were those of Muslim and adivasi girls, both eighteen years of age or less at the time they were assaulted.

- *On October 22, 2005, Prabhawati, a Dalit woman in Mirzapur, U.P., was admitted to a local hospital with 90 per cent burns. The previous Thursday, the day of the panchayat vote, she had been dragged out of her house by men of her own caste who wanted her to withdraw her candidacy. Her assailants poured kerosene over her and lit a bonfire to mock the "empowerment" of low-caste women. Although Prabhawati's husband filed an FIR with the police station immediately, not a single arrest had been made even three days later.* (Sunday Times of India, *23.10.05)*
- *Drive into the Meerut-Bijnore-Muzaffarnagar belt and almost every village has a tale to tell of panchayat brutality. If Khalilpur let loose village goons to tie Prabha to an electric pole, beat her black and blue and shave her head because she had chosen to spend a night with a relative, Johri village banned the marriage of Yashpal's daughter on the ground that it violated caste norms. The panchayat here, by its own admission, has let off rapists and murderers after levying a fine. The village pradhan, Raghuraj Singh, confirmed that the body of an infant, poisoned by her mother, was quietly disposed of at midnight. A rapist was let off after he paid a fine of Rs. 25,000. Kukra is well-known for exploiting the Imrana episode for money and media attention, and then abandoning her to fight her sister-in-law in court.* (Hindustan Times, *12.10.05)*

IV

Caste panchayats are illegal and unconstitutional, often ensure that the police do not interfere in their functioning, and for some villages like Johri in Baghpat (U.P.) not a single policeman has set foot in it for the last five years. In Bijnore, when Prabha was being beaten senseless, the beat constable was a mute witness. Caste panchayats "succeed" because they dispense with due process and take immediate action—and because the victims are helpless. Furthermore, they "spare" both victim and perpetrator from exploitation and humiliation at the hands of the police, and from the corruption of the system.

In May–June 1988, jawans of the Assam Rifles indulged in the gang-rape and molestation of tribal women in Ujan Maidan, a remote village in Tripura. The Congress (I)—TUJS government in the state as well as the Assam Rifles High Command denied that any atrocities had taken place at all, alleging that the charges were intended to malign and discredit the government. Five separate enquiries—by the state police, the local police, the Criminal Investigation Department, the district magistrate and the Assam Rifles—were announced, and all five concluded that the charges were fabricated. However, in July 1990, the All India Democratic Women's Association (AIDWA) presented a memorandum to a parliamentary team visiting Tripura, in which they listed the names of 145 women who had been raped over a period of 20 months between 1988 and 1990. Tribals and Muslims were specially targetted.[20]

Caste and communal violence against women, and violence by the state and armed forces have occurred with brutal and increasing frequency in India over the period under review. Surat (1992–93), Gujarat (2002), Kashmir, Tripura, Nagaland, Manipur, Bombay...Retaliatory, pre-emptive, retributive or plain old sexual violence against women of the Other, against female relatives or companions of so-called "terrorists" or "extremists", and against women militants themselves have become numbingly routine. State complicity in collective, communal sexual violence against women (usually Muslim women) either through direct involvement or through inaction, sanctions such violence against its own citizens in the same way that caste groups violate their own members, and family violence is directed at its own women.[21]

The situation of adivasi women is one that needs to be foregrounded as well. The simultaneous derogation of their rights within communities and vis-à-vis the state and hegemonic non-tribal communities, is one that bears reiteration. The systematic dispossession of the approximately 67 million adivasi people has assumed genocidal proportions over the past five decades. If displacement is one of the issues, violence against girls and women is a major concern as well. A recent study identified eight categories of perpetrators of physical and sexual assault in Tamil Nadu, in which forest officials ranked second.[22] In cases where perpetrators were non-tribals, estate managers, private security on estates, etc., the fact of police complicity through non-registration of cases was evident. Over 300 women in over a quarter of the villages spread across seven districts in Tamil Nadu were forcibly sterilized.[23] Apart from the systematic deployment of violence, adivasi women in "disturbed" areas are the target of state repression, often taken into custody in the absence of husbands or for interrogation to police stations in brazen violation of procedural prescriptions. The violence of the state and non-adivasi communities on the one hand, and the retreat into "customary" community-based mechanisms of "justice" on the other, locks adivasi women into situations of extreme vulnerability and destitution, epitomized by Mathura and Maki Bui.[24]

Gender within caste society is defined and structured in such a manner that the "manhood" of the caste is defined both by the degree of control men exercise over women, and the degree of passivity (and complicity) of the women of the caste. By the same token, demonstrating control by humiliating women of another caste is a sure-fire way of reducing the "manhood" of those castes.[25] Spaces, domestic and public, are similarly structured along lines of caste and gender. The Scheduled Castes and Scheduled Tribes (Prevention of Atrocities) Act, 1989, recognizes the gendered nature of caste experience, especially for Dalit women. In the definition of atrocity therefore, it makes explicit mention of the kinds of violence that women may be subjected to—sexual assault, consensual intercourse using threat from a position of dominance, stripping and parading naked are acts which fall within the meaning of atrocity in the law.

V

As Kumkum Sangari has said,

> Violence is a foundational and systemic feature of all contemporary patriarchies. [They] rest equally on consent by women, violence against women and legitimating ideolo-

> gies. The fact that there is no full male monopoly of institutional and interpersonal violence, that women can be active agents in inciting and inflicting violence, suggests the obvious: that patriarchies are not the rule of men over women, but systemic structures. Indeed, patriarchies work to undermine solidarities by dividing women within the same family, neighbourhood, caste or class, as well as across classes, castes and religions.[26]

Empirical and analytical research in India has established quite clearly that violence against women is systemically, rather than incidentally, engendered. Patriarchal power and privilege operate through socially and culturally sanctioned institutions and structures that tacitly endorse the practice of violence in order to remain dominant. Males of all castes and classes dominate and subjugate their women, even though they themselves may be oppressed by men (and women) of higher castes and classes. The interlocking, or dovetailing, of public and private patriarchies means that women experience linked or connected forms of violence that extend from the home to the street and on to the battlefield.

Within marriage and family, the normative practice of endogamous marriage, at a very young age, serves to perpetuate class and caste hierarchies and religious and ethnic communities. These are ensured through a strict, and often violent, policing of women's mobility and sexuality, and of their reproductive capacities. An across-the-board preference for sons, admittedly more evident in the north and east of the country than in the south and west, exacerbates women's subordinate status as well as their vulnerability. Cultural and social customs generally militate against natal families coming to the aid of their daughters or providing them with shelter from domestic abuse or battery. The overwhelming pressure for early arranged marriages and the stigma attached to divorce, coupled with women's economic dependence, more or less guarantees their submission to routinised, everyday violence in the home; over time it is internalized by them (and others) as being part and parcel of women's condition, to be borne with fortitude and in silence.

Violence within the family is inscribed, open and visible at different levels—symbolically,[27] psychologically[28] and physically through practices of overt and systematic cruelty. There is an acknowledgement that certain categories of kin are opposed in interest and adversarial conduct, and this is normalized within kinship systems. This had led to the deployment of violence and strengthened practices of impunity within families and communities. In the law, provisions of mental and physical cruelty in marriage and the banning of sex determination tests acknowledge this habit of familial violence. The fairly widespread practice of sexual abuse—of male and female children within families—a critical dimension of violence, is recognized as a reality cross-culturally (for instance, as evident in the UN Child Rights Convention) but has not yet begun to figure significantly in theorizing violence within the family. While dowry, marriage and consent, inheritance, maintenance and divorce and spousal violence have been acted upon through campaigns and legislation, "honour" crimes—a cultural expression of the convergence between the patriarchal, heterosexual family and customary law—continue to challenge the boundaries of activism, as the recent case of Maimun demonstrates.[29] The regulation of women's sexuality is a matter of culture and the medium of regulation is violence, ranging from forced marriage to so-called "honour" killings, offences which reify the fact that the family must be a site of reproductive sexuality for communities and must maintain law and order within communities, and by extension, in society.

Son preference, albeit more prevalent among the majority Hindu community than among Muslims or Christians in India, is itself based on perceived advantages and deeply entrenched biases in favour of male children for the performance of ritual and religious ceremonies, as well as for providing economic and social security in a society that offers little of either to its citizens. The necessity of male progeny for continuing the patrilineal line are an additional powerful factor in maintaining son preference and increasing the unwanted "costs" of bearing and rearing dauthers. The heaviest burden is that of providing a suitable, often crushing, dowry in order to secure their marriages. When this is considered to have fallen short of expectations by the groom and his family, dowry murders may, and often do, ensue. One way of avoiding this high cost, as well as ensuring that only male children are born, is to eliminate the girl child before she is born. This violence-in-the-womb is a relatively new but pernicious way of controlling women's reproduction and reinforcing their inferior status. It also ensures that family or group control over the foetus is directly linked to reproducing the legitimate community, as desired.[30]

Consequently, cross-caste or cross-community and inter-faith marriages are proscribed, and sometimes violently dealt with. Such violence may be enacted privately, by family members alone, against errant boys and/or girls, or publicly, together with caste panchayats and village elders or elites. This slippage, or easy transition, between family and social groups, and from the private into the public sphere serves to, both, blur the distinction between the two as well as strengthen the power of class, caste and community patriarchies and sanction the use of violence in their service. The significant fact of "resolving" (if it can be called that) such transgressions by caste and village panchayats is that they *displace the justice-dispensing function of the state* and elevate informal or non-state systems of justice into "customary" practice, recognized by law.[31] Moreover, such systems rarely acknowledge the principle of gender or social equality, and almost invariably reinforce patriarchal norms. (In one sensational instance of this in India in 2005, Muslim clerics issued a fatwa against a woman who was raped by her father-in-law, demanding that she marry the man because she was now "mother" to her husband!) Sangari further maintains that the arrogation of adjudicatory power by these informal systems reduces the distinction between public and private, because it is "sanctioned" by the institutions of the state through inaction.[32] But not only; the state itself secures patriarchal privilege by simultaneously upholding a regime of religion-based, discriminatory personal laws, as well as refraining from "interfering" in the domestic sphere should violence take place within it. This is exacerbated by the fact that those very patriarchal attitudes and discriminatory practices that characterize unequal gender relations in the domestic sphere, are reproduced in the public one. Nussbaum notes that for the majority of women, public space simply does not exist or exists mostly in the abstract, for two important reasons: one, because their entry into it is strictly regulated by male authority, and two, because even those very few women who do access it, rarely do so as true equals.[33]

The liberal formulation that people are rights-bearing individuals pursuing their interests in civil society, takes the separation of the private and public domains for granted. Yet, as Wendy Brown has argued,

> In classical liberal formulations, rights do not apply in (the private) sphere; rather, this realm is constructed as governed by norms of duty, love and custom, in addition to nature, and . . . till recently, has been largely shielded from the reach of law. This is why it has been so difficult to establish marital rape as rape, wife battering as battery or child abuse as abuse.[34]

She concludes thus, that "masculinism lies at the heart of the liberal formulation of political and civil subjects and rights; the liberal subject is a man who moves freely between family and civil society, bearing prerogative in the former and rights in the latter."[35]

Brown takes this argument further by maintaining that state power is "no more gender neutral than it is neutral with regard to class and race" (or caste, in India's case), so that appeals made to the state by women for greater legal protection involve "seeking protection *from* masculinist institutions *against* men"—usually a fraught proposition.[36] This has been demonstrated again and again by women's experiences with institutions like the police and judiciary when it comes to obtaining redressal and justice for violence perpetrated against them. In India, convictions for rape are as low as five per cent of cases reported; and for dowry deaths, far, far less. Yet, according to the National Crime Records Bureau, 2004, there is one rape every 29 minutes in India; one molestation every 15 minutes; and one crime against women every three minutes. (*Indian Express*, April 15, 2006.)

For the women's movement, the most intractable form of violence against women is the collectivized sexual violence by communities, agents of the state and caste groups who think of themselves as being above the law, either because they enjoy immunity, like the armed forces; because they arrogate adjudicatory power to themselves like the caste panchayats; or because they employ others to do the job, like Narendra Modi's government in Gujarat in 2002. Paradoxically, this form of violence is unabashedly public, brazenly sexual and undeniably criminal. Yet it has been normalized.

The ideological, de facto and tacit complicity of the state in violence against women is compounded by its own crimes of sexual violence committed by its agencies—the armed forces or custodial institutions—especially in situations of conflict, insurgency or civil unrest. In the period under review, exhaustive documentation is available of the most brutal rapes and sexual violations of women by the armed forces in Kashmir and all the states of the north-east, and active instigation of it by government functionaries in Gujarat in 2002 (see Ch. 5 for a detailed discussion of this). Exercising its prerogative as the defender of "national security" and maintainer of "law and order", the state claims immunity from the law for crimes committed in the line of duty, or in defence of the nation. This is what Wendy Brown calls "prerogative power, the state's 'legitimate' arbitrary aspect"—its legitimate arbitrary power in policy making, and monopolies of internal and external violence in the police and military.[37] But it is legitimate by virtue of being extra-legal, by exempting itself as the "protective" state from being liable for sexual crimes against women. State violence against women in India is also communalized and tribalized. In Kashmir, it is Muslim women who have been the victims of rape by the armed or border security forces; in Nagaland, Manipur and Mizoram, tribal and Christian women have been similarly sexually violated for all the time that the region has been under military occupation. This raises some grave concerns with regard to not only the state's "masculinism" but its "communalism" and, by implication, casteism.

The Indian state's prerogative, communal aspect, post-Partition, was manifestly evident in its Operation Recovery, through which it "recovered" Hindu and Muslim women and male children who had been abducted during and after the division of India. Feminist analyses of this programme have delineated how the state, in its role as *parens patriae*, arrogated extra-legal, arbitrary police and judicial powers to itself through legislation, with regard to the forcible recovery of adult women, in clear violation of their civil rights as citizens of a secular state. By definition, the Recovery programme was communal, masculinist and patriarchal. It was also violent. It was communal because it concerned itself only with the abduction and forcible conversion and marriage of Hindu, Sikh and Muslim women by men of the "other" community; the rape or abduction of women by men of their own community formed no part of this programme. In other words, rape and abduction were regarded as "heinous offences" only because—and when—they were communalized. It was violent because it gave the police enormous powers of search and seizure, and engaged in actual physical violence while recoveries were being made. And it was arbitrary with regard to its definition of "abduction"; to disputed cases; and, above all, in its complete suspension of any right to redress on the part of the women or their families.[38] Conversely—or, predictably—because the rape, sexual violation and murder of women in Gujarat in 2002 was restricted to Muslims, it was carried out with impunity, hardly qualifying as a crime.

As the International Initiative for Justice observed in the context of Gujarat, [w]hile the torture of men generally creates empathy and solidarity among the targeted community, the sexualized torture of women is particularly destructive to patriarchal notions of female honour.[39] The critical aspect of this violence is that it was rationalized in terms of the ideology of *hindutva*. In Tanika Sarkar's words:

> The pattern of cruelty suggests three things. One, the woman's body was a site of almost inexhaustible violence, with infinitely plural and innovative forms of torture. Second, their sexual and reproductive organs were attacked with a special savagery. Third their children, born and unborn, shared the attacks and were killed before their eyes.[40]

The pattern itself suggests that the violence was neither sporadic nor spontaneous, but targeted, pre-planned and systematic. The mere possibility of violence on the scale that Gujarat witnessed pointed to the active participation of state actors through participation in violence in some places and refusal to offer protection in others, both responses converging to provide the necessary impunity to perpetrators.

This throws up a particularly poignant challenge to feminists and makes for a strange predicament: if the state itself violates the law instead of upholding it; if, indeed, it places itself above the law, can the law and other state institutions be relied upon to redress injury rather than perpetrate it? When what Upendra Baxi characterizes as a "democidal" state actively promotes a rape culture (as it did in Gujarat 2002) "whereby brutal collective sexual assaults on women remain enclosed in contrived and escalating orders of impunity",[41] from whom is protection to be sought? If, as Wendy Brown has said,

> The institutions, practices and discourses of the state are as inextricably, however differently, bound up with the prerogatives of manhood in a male dominant society, as they are with capital and class in a capitalist society and with white supremacy in a racist society, what are the implications for feminist politics?[42]

Specifically, for the purposes of our discussion, what are the implications for both feminist analysis and action regarding violence against women?

From the very first incidents of collective, state and communal violence against women—Bhagalpur, Surat, Deorala, Bombay, Kashmir, Tripura, Nagaland, Manipur, Gujarat—women's groups have reported, documented and presented detailed accounts of the violence, generally at variance with official versions of the events. They have organized public hearings and citizens' tribunals; petitioned the courts, including the Supreme Court; approached state commissions, the National Commission for Women (NCW) and the National Human Rights Commission (NHRC); intervened in reporting processes on human rights at the international level, and of course, exposed the violence and its perpetrators through the media and its own publications. In almost every instance mentioned above, it was women's groups who were the first to initiate independent investigations and record the survivors' statements or testimonies; and it was their painstaking piecing together of the evidence and sequence of events that established the complicity and culpability of the state, the bureaucracy or the armed forces. Or, indeed, the organized lumpen of the Hindu Right—or Left—and dominant sections of civil society. In fact, their reports and investigations remain the only available authentic data on such sexual violence against women, since no "official" reports (including, on occasion, those of the NCW) unequivocally assign culpability to the state and law-enforcing agencies.

The feminist response in terms of using international conventions, however, has probably been more productive. The periodic reports of the government on the implementation of CEDAW and the mobilizing of women's groups around reporting practices of violence from different regions in the country; the process of lobbying for the inclusion of caste within the definition of race and the efforts of the National Federation of Dalit Women to strike a different note that mapped the specificity of Dalit women's experiences; the use of the Due Diligence provision to attract the Rome Statute with reference to the violence in Gujarat in 2002; the use of the definition of "Crimes against Humanity" in the Rome Statute to describe what was happening to the sex ratio in the country, are a few examples of the range of feminist interventions to call states and nations to account. Drawing on the definition of racial discrimination in Article 1 of the Convention on the Elimination of Racial Discrimination, the National Federation of Dalit Women asserted in the Durban process that discrimination based on caste is indeed a specific form of racism, intertwined with gender, since Dalit women

> face targeted violence from state actors and powerful members of dominant castes and communities especially in the case of rape, mutilation and death; they face discrimination in the payment of unequal wages and gender violence at the workplace that includes fields [as agricultural labourers], on the streets [as manual scavengers and garbage pickers], in homes [as domestic workers], and through religious custom . . .[43]

In the course of organizing around issues of violence and coping with shifts in the patterns of violence along lines of ethnicity, religion, community, caste, class and sexual orientation, women's groups have discovered that their own location is not unrelated to their work with communities, especially around issues of customary and inter-group violence. While the campaigns around Rameeza and Mathura resulted in making issues of violence against women visible in radically different ways, the fact of their identity as Muslim and adivasi women, respectively, only entered the account in a descriptive fashion; intersectional analyses that read caste/community/tribe with gender-based discrimination only came later. The question of intersectionality and identity was raised in the first instance by women in the context of the uniform civil code, while the issue of caste and gender figured more centrally while theorising violence.

Consequently, there have been intense conversations around issues of dominance and hegemony within fields of feminist organizing. This has resulted in the creation of specific networks that attempt to address questions of identity and belonging, and in positioning articulations of women's rights within these larger questions. The Manifesto of the National Federation of Dalit Women, for instance, sets it apart from the autonomous women's movement in India on one side, and "male-dominated secular and progressive movements", including the Dalit movement, on the other—underscoring the need for critical reflection on caste-based discrimination *and* the violence inflicted on Dalit women.[44]

VI

To summarise the foregoing, campaigning for the right to *life* has been critical to feminist organizing around violence against women. In the early 1980s, women's groups theorised the patriarchal bases of the criminal justice system and sought legal reform as a way of providing effective remedy and redress for women. The legislations that extended the scope of rape and domestic violence, both definitionally and procedurally, are a case in point. Chapter 2 will examine the trajectory of legal reform in the light of feminist campaigns across three decades.

The vibrancy of the women's movement derives from the rich tapestry of protest that has been created over the years. The fashioning of protest in ever new ways is largely responsible for sustaining struggles against violence despite the lack of visible victory over three decades. Chapter 3 will examine some alternative forms of protest that have captured the imagination of hundreds across the country.

Feminist movements began in the first instance with

consciousness-raising. This project needed to move in new directions if women were to be freed from systemic and systematic violence. Consciousness-raising moved into the media, among professionals, officers in state institutions and elected representatives, to name a few. Chapter 4 recapitulates some experiences of feminist intervention from different parts of the country.

A decade after new legal provisions with greater protections had been put in place, neither the position nor the condition of women had altered significantly. A major hurdle was the fact that the habits of impunity, especially in the state and dominant sections, as well as the unabashed convergence of interests between the two undermined any potential that legal reform might have had. The existence of laws on paper did not guarantee their conscientious implementation, nor did it mean that there had been any dent in the ideology of the state vis-à-vis women. Chapter 5 looks at major episodes of collective violence against women, and the character and magnitude of impunity despite the existence of beneficial legislation.

Notes & references

[1] Vibhuti Patel, "Women's Action Groups and the State Machinery", in Maithreyi Krishnaraj (ed.), *Women and Violence: A Country Report* (Bombay: SNDT, 1991) p. 154.

[2] A letter, in Bengali, was rceived by the Counsel Club, Calcutta, after its address was published in the *Ananda Bazar Patrika* on April 3, 1999. The letter was undated, with no address given and an indistinct postmark. It was signed by a woman named NP, bidding farewell to her family and society. Quoted in Bina Fernandez (ed.), *Humjinsi: A Resource Book on Lesbian, Gay and Bisexual Rights in India* (Revised Edition, Bombay: India Centre for Human Rights and Law), 2002.

[3] Cited in the CEDAW Alternative Report submitted to the UN CEDAW Committee, 2006.

[4] For a detailed discussion of this event, see Chapter 5 in this monograph.

[5] See Gail Omvedt, *Violence Against Women: New Movements and New Theories in India* for a cogent review of theories of violence against women (New Delhi: Kali for Women, 1990, 2000).

[6] Gail Omvedt, op. cit., p. 16.

[7] Nandita Gandhi and Nandita Shah, *The Issues at Stake: Theory and Practice in the Contemporary Women's Movement in India* (New Delhi: Kali for Women, 1992), p. 94.

[8] Ibid., p. 95.

[9] *Bharwada Bhoginbhai Hirjibhai* AIR 1983 SC 753.

[10] The Criminal Law (Amendment) Act, 2006 incorporated most suggestions made, barring the two points on which it differed, i.e., consent and marital rape.

[11] Flavia Agnes, *Feminist Jurisprudence: Contemporary Concerns* (Bombay: Majlis, 2003), pp. 8–9.

[12] For a harrowing and damning account of this see Syeda S. Hameed, *They Hang: Twelve Women in My Portrait Gallery* (New Delhi: Women Unlimited, 2006).

[13] Gandhi and Shah, op. cit., p. 267.

[14] Ibid., p. 268.

[15] Sharifa, personal communication; and Gandhi and Shah, op. cit., for examples from other parts of the country.

[16] See especially Leela Visaria, Nishi Mitra, Veena Poonacha and Divya Pandey, *Domestic Violence in India: A Summary Report of Three Studies*, vol. 1, International Center for Research on Women, Washington, D.C., 1999. Also the *National Family Health Survey* (Second Round), 1998–91; and assorted reports by the Centre for Women's Development Studies, Centre for Social Research, the Lawyers' Collective, and Sakshi (all New Delhi). Also Zoya Hasan and Ritu Menon, *Unequal Citizens: A Study of Muslim Women in India* (New Delhi: Oxford University Press, 2004).
[17] *Mr. Justice Muktadar Commission of Enquiry in the Matter of Detention of Ahmed Hussain and Rameeza Bee, Death of Ahmed Hussain, Alleged Molestation of Rameeza Bee, etc,* May 1978.
[18] *Tukaram vs. State of Maharashtra,* AIR 1979 SC 185.
[19] Pratiksha Baxi, "The Medicalisation of Consent and Falsity: The Figure of the *Habitue* in Indian Rape Law" in Kalpana Kannabiran (ed.), *The Violence of Normal Times: Essays on Women's Lived Realities* (New Delhi: Women Unlimited, 2005).
[20] For a detailed discussion on this see Brinda Karat and Indu Agnihotri, "Violence Against Women", paper presented at the VIth National Conference on Women's Studies, Mysore, 1993.
[21] Kumkum Sangari, "Gendered Violence: The Discourses of Culture and Tradition", in Radhika Coomaraswamy & Nimanthi Rajasingham, *Contested Terrains: Gender, Violence and Representation in South Asia* (New Delhi & Colombo: Women Unlimited & International Center for Ethnic Studies), forthcoming.
[22] Aloysius Irudayam and Jayshree P. Mangubhai, *Adivasis Speak Out: Atrocities against Adivasis in Tamil Nadu* (Tamil Nadu: Village Reconstruction and Development Project, 2003).
[23] Ibid.
[24] *Tukaram vs. State of Maharashtra,* 1979-SCC (Cri) 381, popularly known as the Mathura judgement. Maki Bui was a Ho woman on whose behalf the feminist magazine, *Manushi,* filed a petition in the Supreme Court of India seeking to overturn the denial of equal inheritance rights to women of the Ho tribe. For a detailed account of the case see Madhu Kishwar, *Off the Beaten Track: Rethinking Gender Justice for Women* (New Delhi: Oxford University Press, 1999).
[25] Kalpana Kannabiran and Vasanth Kannabiran, "Caste and

Gender: Understanding the Dynamic of Power and Violence", *Economic and Political Weekly*, September 14, 1991.

[26] Kumkum Sangari, "Gendered Violence," op. cit.

[27] Pierre Bourdieu, *Outline of a Theory of Practice* [trans. Richard Nice] (Cambridge: Cambridge University Press, 1977).

[28] Sudhir Kakar, "Some Unconscious Aspects of Ethnic Violence in India," in Veena Das (ed.), *Mirrors of Violence: Communities, Riots and Survivors in South Asia* (New Delhi: Oxford University Press, 1990).

[29] Syeda S. Hameed, *They Hang: Twelve Women in My Portrait Gallery* op. cit.

[30] See chapter 2 in this monograph for an expanded discussion on the pre-birth elimination of female foetuses.

[31] A point made forcefully by feminist lawyer, Indira Jaising, in a personal communication.

[32] Sangari, op. cit.

[33] Martha Nussbaum, in Zoya Hasan, E. Sridharan, R. Sudarshan (eds.), *India's Living Constitution: Ideas, Practices and Controversies* (New Delhi: Permanent Black, 2002), p. 258.

[34] Wendy Brown, *States of Injury: Power and Freedom in Late Modernity* (New Jersey: Princeton University Press, 1995), p. 181.

[35] Ibid., p. 182.

[36] Ibid., p. 171.

[37] Ibid., p. 176.

[38] For an exhaustive elaboration of this see Ritu Menon & Kamla Bhasin, *Borders & Boundaries: Women in India's Partition* (New Delhi: Kali for Women, 1998, 2000); Urvashi Butalia, *The Other Side of Silence: Voices from the Partition of India* (New Delhi: Viking, 1998); and Kamla Patel, *Torn from the Roots: A Partition Memoir* (New Delhi: Women Unlimited, 2006).

[39] *Threatened Existence: A Feminist Analysis of the Genocide in Gujarat*, Report by the International Initiative for Justice (IIJ), December 2003.

[40] Tanika Sarkar, "Semiotics of Terror: Muslim Women and Children in Hindu Rashtra," *Economic and Political Weekly*, July 13, 2002.

[41] Upendra Baxi, "The Gujarat Catastrophe: Notes on Reading

Politics as Democidal Rape," in Kalpana Kannabiran (ed.), *The Violence of Normal Times*, op. cit., p. 341.

[42] Wendy Brown, op. cit., p. 169.

[43] National Federation of Dalit Women, NGO Declaration on Gender and Racism, Racial Discrimination, Xenophobia and Related Intolerance, World Conference Against Racism, 28 August–7 September 2001, Durban, South Africa.

[44] See also Vimal Thorat, "Dalit women have been left behind by the Dalit movement and the women's movement," *Communalism Combat*, May 2001.

2 Judicial and Legislative Action

Kalpana Kannabiran

VIOLENCE against women locks women of different classes, castes and communities into multiple intersecting axes of inequality and discrimination that radiate over a wide spectrum—from social and economic life to political inequality—tying women of different classes together through the similarity of their experiences as women, yet holding them apart in almost unbridgeable ways through the differences in their experiences as members of different social classes.

Public discourse on violence is characterized by a strong moral disapproval of perpetrators of violence. And yet, as Patricia Viseur Sellers has argued, the problem is that this disapproval falls highly selectively.[1] First, it is often assumed that the danger of violence lies exclusively in its use by dissidents, yet figures from across the world demonstrate quite clearly that authorities are greater perpetrators of violence. Second, the violence of normal times is neither equally condemned nor even equally recognized. Nor do people try to eradicate it.[2] It is here that violence against women is deeply embedded, and because it is the greater part of all violence against them, it carries with it the guarantee of impunity, irrespective of penal, punitive or constitutional safeguards. Sudden conflagrations of violence, violent upsurges, must then be understood in the context of this steady, ever present, violence of normal times.

The complete normalization of sexual, domestic, communal and public violence against women has forced a re-examination of the ways in which it is welded to the question of rights. Force and violence—the policing of culture, the cry of nationalism and patriotism, matters of family honour and war—etch almost identical inscriptions on women's bodies through rape, physical assault, "honour" killings, and the straightforward denial of equality claims. From the stories of Partition to Gujarat in 2002, from the women who were forced onto their husbands' pyres in nineteenth century Bengal to Roop Kanwar's sati in North India, there has been a persistence of violence against women, despite all safeguards and instrumentalities of governmental and intergovernmental bodies. Do we look at this as the twilight of women's rights or as the darkness before a new dawn?[3]

Sexual terrorism, to use Cheris Kramarae's term, is used to silence women and subjugate them through the systematic use and constant threat of violence,[4] and is always part of larger political projects that hinge on the absolute appropriation of women's bodies. This terrorism, an intrinsic part of male dominance and social inequality, is established through acts of physical aggression, but equally if not more powerfully, through words. Shame, guilt, honour, chastity, immorality, virginity, lust, bestiality, ravishment, modesty, outrage, molestation, penetration, consent, rape, are words that by themselves, through usage alone, constitute sexual terrorism; they are also deeply entrenched in the discourses of the state. Moreover, this condition intersects with other ongoing hegemonic enterprises to produce a complex discursive field within which women's rights—especially against rape and violence—are articulated.

In a context where the systematic exclusion of women is a norm in political and public life, redefining the "public" and the "normal" is an important undertaking. Using the provisions of international instruments to demarcate and set new standards becomes a critical strategy for combating violence and forcing state action in order to protect women from violence in various "private" spheres. Over the past fifteen years especially, women's groups in India have found it useful to build anti-violence campaigns around international conventions, as a way of prising open the private sphere to public scrutiny and public law in more effective ways. Clearly this is easier said than done in a country where even judges believe that bringing law enforcement into the family is like being a bull in a china shop. Yet, at the same time, by forcing the judiciary and legislature to reckon with international standards as a measure of their own commitment to a broad-based notion of human rights in civil society, women's groups in India have achieved some significant gains on paper; the enactment of legislation or the drafting of new legislation may not in itself be a sign of change on the ground, but it certainly marks a discursive shift that interrogates the "normalcy" of the violence of normal times.

This chapter will focus on interactions between the judiciary and feminists/ women's rights activists, and look at specific legal initiatives in the area of violence against women, examining legal provisions, statutory interpretation and feminist engagements with formal law.

Sexual harassment at the workplace

The 1997 Supreme Court judgement on sexual harassment in *Vishaka*[5] has been hailed by women's groups all over the country as a milestone in a long drawn-out struggle for gender justice. A survey conducted by Sanhita, a Calcutta-based women's group, revealed that a large number of women faced some form or other of sexual harassment at the workplace, while an even larger number work under the threat, or perpetual fear, of being sexually harassed. The Vishaka judgement set out a series of guidelines for dealing with such harassment, making employers and institutions responsible for implementing both preventive and remedial measures. For the first time in judicial history, the court recognized sexual harassment at the workplace as a recurring phenomenon. By the court's own admission, it was found necessary to put this measure in place, given the agenda of the Beijing Platform for Action and the Convention on the Elimination of all Forms of Discrimination Against Women (CEDAW), both of which called for states' parties to ensure safe work environments for women across the world.

In 1992, Bhanwari Devi, a 50 year old Dalit woman employed as a *saathin* in a government programme to combat child marriage in Rajasthan, was gang-raped by five upper caste landlords for "reporting" on child marriages in the village of Bhateri. Through her persistence in pursuing her case at enormous personal cost, Bhanwari epitomizes the struggle of women against violence and injustice. In terms of formal justice, however, Bhanwari still waits, with her rapists acquitted and the state disbelieving her charges. Women's groups used the fact of Bhanwari's vulnerability, deriving from the nature of her employment, to petition the Supreme Court and seek legal redress against sexual harassment at the workplace.[6]

The purpose of the writ petition, filed by them collectively as Vishaka, was to seek "the enforcement of fundamental rights of working women under Articles 14, 19 and 21 of the Constitution of India, in view of the prevailing climate in which the violation of these rights is not uncommon". In the years that followed the Vishaka decision, women's rights groups across the country have lobbied with government and private employers to implement the Supreme Court guidelines, constitute complaints committees and create an atmosphere that is conducive for women to work in, unhindered—i.e., to eliminate hostile work environments—but also to create an atmosphere in which it is possible for women who face harassment to seek effective remedies. While the constitution of the committees and procedures for implementing the guidelines continue to be fraught with problems, there is no doubt that there has been a radical change in the content of public discourse, with people in workplaces forced to commit themselves to dealing effectively with sexual harassment, even if the gains are few in practice.

With respect to women in the unorganized sector, however, the problem remains unaddressed; women workers in free trade zones are one example. In sectors that completely lack transparency and procedure in recruitment, conditions of employment and remuneration, the vulnerability of women workers is compounded by their situation as women, with gender discrimination slipping easily, and often, into sexual harassment, and any resistance or confrontation leading immediately to loss of employment in an already precarious survival scenario. Padmini Swaminathan's work on the condition of women workers in export processing zones demonstrates the interconnections between the denial of fair conditions of work and wages, dehumanising work environments and routinely high levels of sexual harassment, with no checks on the employer and no possible conditions for solidarity among women workers.[7] While the Vishaka judgement represents a landmark feminist intervention, its impact has still to be felt on women's employment in general in the country; the gains are concentrated in a few pockets, restricted largely to cases that come to court, especially those dealing with women in the formal sector or white-collar employment.

Although the Vishaka judgement marked a major reframing of judicial discourse, the shift in understanding sexual harassment at the workplace predated it. The feminist signpost was the 1995 Rupan Deol Bajaj case,[8] which resulted in the norms of "acceptable" behaviour being firmly reinscribed: from frivolous "eve-teasing" to sexual harassment as a *derogation of women's right to dignity.* While the term "sexual harassment" entered usage in 1997, the Bajaj case witnessed the radical application of the archaic "outraging of modesty" provision, preparing the ground for sexual harassment provisions. Rupan Deol Bajaj, an IAS officer in Punjab, was slapped on her bottom in public at an official dinner attended by several senior officers of the Punjab Government. Obstructed from pursuing the case in Punjab, Bajaj finally approached the Supreme Court of India, which found the officer in question, K.P.S. Gill, guilty, and convicted him to a prison term and fine. However, despite a radical application of the legal remedy, the discursive frame within which it was situated is cause for concern.

Up until this point, prosecution in sexual harassment cases relied on legal provisions in the Indian Penal Code, specifically Sections 209 (obscene acts and songs), 354 (assault or criminal force on a woman with the intent to outrage her modesty), and 509 (word, gesture or act intended to insult the modesty of a woman). There have also been cases (though rare) where sexual harassment has been argued with reference to unfair labour practices in the Industrial Disputes Act, Rule 5, Schedule 5.

The only statutory code that uses the term "modesty" is the Indian Penal Code, but it does not define it. Yet, across the board, modesty sits at the core of jurisprudence. Since the Indian Penal Code does not define modesty, which is the crux of Sections 354 and 509, Judges Anand and Mukherjee, in a 1980 case, dwelt at length on dictionary meanings of the word which centered on notions of "womanly propriety", "shame", "chastity", "decency", "decorous in manner and conduct", "freedom from coarseness, indelicacy and indecency", etc.[9] The "inherent bashfulness of women"[10] is a notion that has been reiterated in the Supreme Court for several decades.

The Supreme Court judgement in the Vishaka case altered the framework of this discourse, making such notions appear archaic and uncivilised. This judgement was delivered

> . . . in the absence of enacted law to provide for the effective enforcement of the basic human right of gender equality and guarantee against sexual harassment and abuse [and] in exercise of the power available under Article 32 of the Constitution for the enforcement of fundamental rights [and] would be treated as the law declared by this Court under Article 141 of the Constitution.[11]

For this purpose, sexual harassment includes such unwelcome sexually determined behaviour (whether directly or by implication) as:

(*a*) physical contact and advances;
(*b*) a demand or request for sexual favours;

(*c*) sexually coloured remarks;
(*d*) showing pornography;
(*e*) any other unwelcome physical, verbal or non-verbal conduct of sexual nature.

where any of these acts is committed in circumstances where the victim of such conduct has a reasonable apprehension that, in relation to her employment or work, such conduct can be humiliating and may constitute a health and safety problem. It is discriminatory, for instance, when the woman has reasonable grounds to believe that her objection would disadvantage her in connection with her employment or work, including recruiting or promotion, or when it creates a hostile work environment. Adverse consequences might be visited if the victim does not consent to the conduct in question or raises any objection thereto.

These guidelines were framed from the standpoint of a working class Dalit woman's vulnerability vis-à-vis dominant castes, the police and the state/government. The purpose of the writ petition submitted by Vishaka was to seek

> . . . the enforcement of fundamental rights of working women under Articles 14, 19 and 21 of the Constitution of India in view of the prevailing climate in which the violation of these rights is not uncommon.[12]

Locating gender equality within Article 14 and reiterating that "[t]he fundamental right to carry on any occupation, trade or profession depends on the availability of a 'safe' working environment"; and that the "[r]ight to life means life with dignity",[13] the Vishaka judgement in fact addresses the larger question of gender-based discrimination, of which sexual harassment may or may not be a part. There has been considerable discussion in US courts on whether 'sex' is to be taken to mean gender, or to mean 'sex' in its more popular sense of the sexual act. While the former is perhaps the only way to contextualise and understand the harassment of women at the workplace in an all-encompassing manner, courts in the US, and more recently in India, seem to favour the disaggregation of a complaint into sexual and non-sexual items, thus proving counter-productive to women, mostly for lack of "direct" evidence.[14]

The advantage we have in India with respect to the issue of sexual harassment is the fact that it is up to universities and workplaces to evolve and ratify codes that will ensure greater democratic functioning and transparency. However, it is important not merely to have independent policy statements on sexual harassment which are not justiciable at all, but to build that policy commitment into existing statutory provisions that govern the conduct of employees and employers, teachers and students in establishments; difficult issues of remedy and redress, as well as reasonable opportunity and fair procedures, may thus be resolved more easily.[15]

Sexual harassment is located at the intersection of two trajectories of interpretation to begin with—that of constitutional law with respect to Articles 14, 15 and 16 of the Constitution of India; and that of criminal law, not just with reference to Section 354 (outraging the modesty of a woman) but also Sections 375 and 376 (rape)—because anything that "falls short of rape" is "outraging modesty". Exploring the complex articulations of gender-based discrimination and, through them, the pervasiveness of "hostile environments" for women in the workplace, would serve to place the Vishaka decision in proper perspective.

To begin with, questions of equality based on sex primarily address the imperatives of those in employment (particularly in the formal sector) and property-owning classes; women from the informal sector and casual employment are absent from the field of sexual harassment redress and remedy. In other words, there is a common ground that the issue of sexual harassment inhabits with equality. The range of feminist legal writing on anti-discrimination jurisprudence draws from the understanding that (*a*) discrimination can mean imposing conditions or setting the norm outside the normal experience of an entire class, and then measuring that class against the norm; and (*b*) that sex is a relational category that functions always in combination with other factors which may or may not be explicit.[16]

Yet the jurisprudence on discrimination against women is replete with equivocations that reflect an inability to grasp its complexity. There is, for instance, an assumption that "the function of females in Indian society is that of housewives," which then goes on to structure the judicial view of entitlements and protections. This leads to a series of justifications for discrimination—either in terms of "exonerating them" from "onerous and petty responsibilities" like receiving notices;[17] classifying the jobs they will "naturally" perform well (for instance, teaching primary school rather than high school children [irrespective of their qualifications and experience])[18]; or terminating their services because they may be less efficient after marriage.[19]

The idea that "the function of females in Indian society is that of housewives," rhetorically absents women from the material contexts of work, while translating demands for entitlements in paid work into the fuzzy area of unpaid work as a function of "love", a world that is completely unregulated, uncompensated and unprotected from exploitation, dispossession and (especially) sexual assault: "A woman in our country occupies a very high and *respected position in the society as a mother, a wife, a companion and a social worker.*"

While there have been major decisions that have struck down discriminatory provisions in the civil services,[20] and a recognition, at one level, that "[o]ur struggle for national freedom was also a battle against woman's thraldom",[21] the centrality of heterosexual marriage to the definition of womanhood remains a disabling factor in women's entitlements to justice and remedies at work.

If the active exclusion of women from the material contexts of paid work is one contributing factor to the creation and sustenance of hostile environments, the "efficiency rule" is the second. Vicki Schultz has demonstrated persuasively the ways in which gender discrimination at work imperceptibly slides into sexual harassment at the workplace.[22] Case law on employment-related discrimination in India is rich with instances of this kind of elision. Whether it is the case of a woman qualified to be a superintendent of a jail who is refused promotion because there is no women's jail (and being a woman, she is by definition incapable of controlling rowdy men in custody, "hardened, ribald criminals guilty of heinous crimes of violence and sex . . .")[23]; or the case of the Tamil Nadu government responding to high absenteeism among male teachers in government schools by classifying teachers by sex, asking women teachers to draw on their natural propensity for nurturance and caring in taking care of children from classes 1 to 5, but once they are old enough to learn lessons of citizenship, handing them over to men teachers who have already proved unreliable and irresponsible,[24] "efficiency" for women in formal employment is always bound to gendered stereotypes of caring and natural capacities (read limitations). This validates the practices of exclusion that we spoke of earlier. In this regard, the Military Nursing Service, for example, laid down rules that, in the interests of efficiency, a person could remain in service after marriage only if *she justified her continuance by showing extra efficiency in the years preceding her marriage.* In a 1991 judgement, the Supreme Court ruled that the appellant be given the opportunity to prove her efficiency in the two years subsequent to marriage, and then be discontinued if found inefficient.[25]

Participation in the workforce is structured by common forms of the gender-based division of labour. Familial and communal allocations of gender roles and responsibilities are reproduced and strengthened in the "secular" workspace, excluding women by definition from the constitution of the space itself, as outsiders and intruders who only complicate otherwise harmonious work arrangements, but must nevertheless be accommodated. The process of accommodation is based on the fundamental ideological premise of women being reproducers, primarily, whose contribution is too diffuse to be remunerated or compensated completely or adequately, and whose work, even when it appears similar to men's, is in fact very different because the emotive premises of women's labour are dissimilar. So, similarities of work are deceptive, and dissimilarities conform to gender differences that harmonise with the ideology of the family and of communities. This is then characterized as differentiation, not discrimination. There are a number of cases that demonstrate this kind of thinking, but the one that epitomizes it is the case of the air hostesses. The question of equality seems to hinge on an either/or decision: Does equality demand treating women like men or does it mean treating women specially? Martha Minow[26] argues that there is a deeper problem embedded in this question, and that is

> . . . a work world that treats as the model worker the traditional male employee who has a full-time wife and mother to care for his home and children. The very phrase 'special treatment', when used to describe pregnancy or maternity leave, posits men as the norm and women as different or deviant from that norm. The problem was not women, or pregnancy, but the effort to fit women's experiences and needs into categories forged with men in mind.[27]

Over the years there has been a considerable shift in the ways in which discrimination against women has been understood and interpreted in courts, the Vishaka decision representing a major step forward. However, more deep-seated assumptions about women interrupt the discourse on anti-discrimination, shrinking the space of redress discursively, even as it seems to expand through statutory interpretation.

Domestic violence

Draft article 42 of the Indian Constitution, which was dropped without a debate, stated that:

> The State shall endeavour to secure that marriage shall be based only on the mutual consent of both sexes and shall be maintained through mutual cooperation with the equal rights of husband and wife as a basis. The State shall also recognize that motherhood has a special claim upon its care and protection.[28]

Domestic violence has been a complex and troubling issue for women and girl children, with practices ranging from female foeticide to the commerce of dowry; and the range of abuses that surround it extending to widow immolation and desertion. This makes the family a potentially extremely unsafe place for women—both for those in heterosexual marriage as well as those who place themselves outside the heterosexual norm. In the latter case, recent documentation has shown that while families systematically assault and abuse lesbian and bisexual women, the offence is compounded by collusion with repressive instrumentalities of the state through the use of "insanity" arguments. While international instruments like CEDAW have been brought into Indian legal regimes, its framework has yet to create any impact on the judicial perception of women's rights in relationships, at a day-to-day level.

Time and again the judiciary has drawn attention to the differences between "the west" and India, especially when the issue concerns women.[29] It often argues (explicitly or implicitly) that unlike their "western counterparts," for "tradition-bound Indian women" equality claims are subservient to claims made on them by their communities or culture, Indian culture being the pinnacle. In fact, the idea of mutuality and equality in marriage is neither new nor western, and we have a range of literature from the Constituent Assembly Debates to that of the Self-Respect Movement in Tamil Nadu that bears testimony to the desirability of mutual and equal conjugality.[30]

Where women are concerned, social arrangements are far from neutral; for the law to assume a posture of neutrality with respect to women has far-reaching consequences in terms of discrimination and an undermining of basic rights. Although the Andhra Pradesh High Court did at one point observe that "bare equality of treatment, regardless of the inequality of realities, is neither justice nor homage to constitutional principles,"[31] the judiciary and legislatures have been quick to distance themselves from the question of women's entitlement to security of person and economic security within the conjugal home. They have argued increasingly (in some cases by amending the law) for making cruelty against women under Section 498A (IPC) compoundable, and expressed reluctance (while acknowledging the fact of cruelty) to treat marital rape as a crime.[32] The following excerpt from a judgement of the Andhra Pradesh High Court is illustrative of the current rhetoric on 498A.

> . . . for nothing educated women are approaching the courts for divorce and resorting to proceedings against their in-laws under Section 498A IPC . . . This is nothing but abuse of beneficial provisions intended to save the women from unscrupulous husbands. But it has taken a reverse trend now . . . It is for the Law Commission . . . to make the offence a non-cognizable one and a bailable one so that the ill-educated women of this country and their parents do not misuse the provision to harass innocent people for the sin of

> contacting [sic] marriage with egoistic women. We have no hesitation to hold that if this situation is continued any longer the institution of marriage and the principle one man for one woman will vanish into [thin] air.[33]

There is within case law, a complete disjuncture in the rhetoric that typifies cruelty against wives, where the woman survives and lodges a criminal complaint, and cases where a woman has died consequent on marriage. While there is a marginal increase in the rate of convictions in the latter case, the position of women survivors who resist violence continues to present a major challenge to women's groups; both because of the non-reporting and intractability of these cases, and the difficulty that women survivors face in sustaining cases in court, dealing as they do with a largely hostile legal profession and criminal justice system.

It is useful at this point to re-examine our earlier arguments about the notion of the "hostile environment" put forth in *Vishaka.* The core of the argument has to do with the structuring of spaces—physical, intellectual and emotional—in ways that entrench ideologies of subordination and the appropriation of women's labour and bodies in inevitably violent ways.[34] A brief review of reported cases of dowry-related violence between the years 1995–2004 is instructive. Although the number of women dying in matrimonial homes remains alarmingly high—poisoned, burnt, battered, drowned, shot, hanged and strangled within the "safe" confines of the family—we see a marginal increase in convictions where women have died gruesome deaths, and a perceptible shift in the judicial conscience. This impact is not as perceptible, however, in cases where the woman escapes the

Patterns and variations in sentencing in trial and appellate courts in randomly selected decisions, 1995–2004

CONVICTIONS				ACQUITTALS			
Trial/Sessions Court Confirmed		*Trial/Sessions Court Reversed*		*Trial/Sessions Court Confirmed*		*Trial/Sessions Court Reversed*	
High Court	*Supreme Court*	*High Court*	*Supreme Court*	*High Court*	*Supreme Court*	*High Court*	*Supreme Court*
31	8	6	–	9	–	27	1

The slight discrepancy in total number of cases is due to cases which did not go up in appeal.

cruelty of the matrimonial home. In that sense the objective of CEDAW remains unattained, since it is intended to further the interests of women who stay alive to enjoy a world free of discrimination.

While most violence that women are subjected to within the matrimonial home is premeditated and intentional, *mens rea* is not read into the murder of wives in the same way as it is in murder per se. The familial relationship is always a mitigating factor in sentencing policy, although in fact this relationship renders these women more vulnerable to assault. In understanding violence against women, especially in the context of legal remedy and redress, it is necessary to address questions of intent and motive and the notion of the "guilty mind", with the same assiduousness as that which addresses questions of evidence, particularly corroboration, in cases of sexual assault.

Sex selective abortion

Sex ratios are a good indicator of gender equality in societies at any given point of time. In general they are an outcome of four different factors: differentials in mortality; sex selective migration; sex ratio at birth; and sex differentials in population enumeration. The 2001 Census Report of India shows a general increase in the sex ratio, but an alarming and sharp decline, by 18 points, in child sex ratio in the age group of 0–6 years. This decline is so widespread that of the 28 states and Union Territories in the country, only four states—Kerala, Tripura, Mizoram and Sikkim—and one Union Territory, Lakshadweep, registered an increase. By inference, this means that these are the only areas in the country that are free from the socially degenerative practice of eliminating girl foetuses and children. States and Union Territories that have shown a sharp decline in sex ratio are Punjab (–82), Haryana (–59), Himachal Pradesh (–54), Gujarat (–50), Chandigarh (–54), and Delhi (–50), although these are the very states that display high indices of economic development; and there are 122 districts in over 14 states that have a child sex ratio of less than 900.[35] Taking note of this trend CEDAW raised the following query:

> [Q 58]: It is a matter of concern that the sex ratio is getting adverse in India and that, even in an advanced state like Kerala, the sex ratio is getting adverse.
>
> *Response of the Indian Government:* It is a fact that the sex ratio in the country has declined to 927 in 1991 (as against 945 in 1947). This reflects 'son preference' and the historical neglect of women's health problems. However, in Kerala, the sex ratio is not adverse. As per the latest Census figures, Kerala has a sex ratio of 1036 females per thousand males.

Any enactment of national legislation on sex selective abortion must take cognizance of its occurrence in radically new terms in order to effectively combat it, but more importantly to put an end to impunity, which is the hallmark of this practice today. As an immediate measure, it is useful to look at the PNDT Act and the amendments therein, since it is an explicit legislation that addresses the problem of sex selective abortion.

The Pre-Conception & Pre-Natal Diagnostic Testing (Prohibition of Sex Selection) Act has a legal history.

In 1988, the Maharashtra Regulation of Pre-Natal Diagnostic Techniques Act was passed, followed by the Pre-Natal Diagnostic Techniques (Regulation and Prevention of Misuse) Act in 1994, the rules for which were framed in 1996. February 2003 saw the passage of Amendments to the PNDT Act. Between 1998 and 2003, a Bombay-based NGO, Centre for Enquiry into Health and Allied Themes (CEHAT) filed a case in the Supreme Court of India on the implementation of the PNDT Act, the final judgement on which was delivered in September 2003.

The PNDT Act aims at prohibiting sex selection before and after conception, and regulating the use of diagnostic techniques. According to this Act, "sex selection" includes "any procedure, technique, test or anything else for the purpose of ensuring or increasing the probability that the embryo will be of a particular sex". The Act permits the use of pre-natal diagnostic techniques *only* for the purposes specified under the Act. These are: the detection of chromosomal abnormalities; genetic metabolic diseases; haemoglobinopathies; sex-linked genetic diseases; congenital abnormalities; other abnormalities or diseases as specified by the Central Supervisory Board.

In addition to the purposes stated, a person can conduct the tests only if he/she is satisfied that the age of the pregnant woman is above 35 years; that she has undergone two or more spontaneous abortions or foetal loss; has been exposed to potentially teratogenic agents such as drugs, radiation, infection or chemicals; that she has a family history of mental retardation or physical deformities such as spasticity or any other genetic disease; or any other condition specified by the

Central Supervisory Board. The key provision in this Act is contained in Section 5 (2), which says that

> No person including the person conducting pre-natal diagnostic procedures shall communicate to the pregnant woman concerned, or her relatives or any other person, the sex of the foetus by words, signs or in any other manner.

Pre-natal diagnostic procedures refer to all gynaecological or obstetrical procedures, including non-invasive ones like ultrasonography and foetoscopy; and invasive procedures like removing samples of amniotic fluid, chorionic villi, blood, any tissue or fluid *of the man or the pregnant woman* for conducting any type of analysis or pre-natal diagnostic tests for selection of sex, both *before and after conception.*

The law works through the registration of ultra sound units, the maintenance of records by them, and implementation of the mandate by medical professionals. In laying down the requirements, the law also details minimum requirements both in terms of competence, skill and the qualification of professionals, as well as the minimum equipment necessary for registering a unit under the Act. In general, genetic counselling centres, genetic laboratories and genetic clinics may be registered under the Act. Any unit so registered is subject to strict scrutiny, must submit periodic reports and maintain scrupulous and accurate records of each case handled by it.

The functions of the Appropriate Authorities under the Act are to grant, suspend or cancel registration; to enforce the standards for genetic counselling centres, genetic clinics and genetic laboratories; investigate complaints of breach of provisions of the Act and the Rules;

take complaints to the court; take appropriate legal action against the use of any sex selection technique by any person or place, either *suo motu* or brought to its attention, and also initiate investigations; create public awareness; supervise the implementation of the Act; recommend modifications in accordance with changes in technology; and take action on the recommendations of the Advisory Committee made after investigation of complaints for suspension or cancellation of registration.

Two cases, both a result of the work done by CEHAT, have so far been filed in the Supreme Court. The first case began with the honourable judge observing that,

> It is an admitted fact that in Indian society, discrimination against the girl child still prevails, maybe because of prevailing uncontrolled dowry system despite the Dowry Prohibition Act, as there is no change in the mind-set, or also because of insufficient education and/or tradition of women being confined to household activities. Sex selection/sex determination further adds to this adversity . . . Advanced technology is increasingly used for removal of foetus (may or may not be seen as commission of murder) but it certainly affects the sex ratio. The misuse of modern science and technology by preventing the birth of a girl child by sex determination before birth and, thereafter, abortion, is evident from the 2001 census figures which reveal greater decline in sex ratio in the 0–6 age group in states like Haryana, Punjab, Maharashtra and Gujarat, which are economically better off.[36]

In order to ensure effective implementation of the Act, the Court issued directions to the central and state governments, as well as to the Appropriate Authorities specified under the Act, to "create public awareness against the practice of pre-natal determination of sex and female foeticide through appropriate releases/programmes in the electronic media"; and implement with "all vigour and zeal" the PNDT Act and the Rules framed in 1996. The Court also prescribed the periodicity for meetings of the Appropriate Authorities, as well as the composition, especially of the Central Supervisory Board, to include public-spirited citizens along with medical practitioners, recognizing that the route to effective implementation did not lie with doctors alone. The significant part of this judgement is that it gave powers of search and seizure to Appropriate Authorities: "Appropriate Authorities are not only empowered to take criminal action, but to search and seize documents, records, objects, etc., of unregistered bodies under Section 30 of the Act."

In addition to seeking directions from the Court for the implementation of the Act, CEHAT also filed a Public Interest Petition,[37] wherein a grievance was made that, in spite of passing the said Act, activities which are prohibited under this Act continue. Doctors (of whom one was a Dr. Malpani) intervened in the matter and filed an affidavit that defended the sex determination test on grounds of "family balancing". Subsequently, another affidavit was filed wherein an apology was tendered, and it was stated that the only wrong committed by them was to continue advertising such an activity on a website. Consequent on this apology, the registration of the Malpani Infertility Clinic was suspended in the public interest, until further orders. However, it was held that this suspension did not affect the right of the petitioners, who were doctors, to continue their practice despite the closure of the diagnostic centre.

The question posed earlier remains: how does one

tackle the problem of social inequality without being caught in the choice and privacy argument?

It is important to make a clear distinction between the woman's right to abortion, and the right of the female foetus against abortion. The standpoint of most doctors on this issue echoes the argument of procreative autonomy that has been developed in US courts.[38] The relevance of the principle of procreative autonomy (and more generally the right to privacy) to the Indian context is specific to the socio-cultural factors of the South Asian region. The argument in favour of procreative autonomy enables the refusal of coercive family planning or population control programmes carried out by the state. However, the problem remains: How does one reconcile, theoretically and experientially, individual women's right to procreative autonomy with their right not to be discriminated against as a class? The issue of abortion therefore forces a synthesis of jurisprudential reasoning with a political reading of rights as they have been articulated in movements. Sex selective abortion, it may be argued, and the more recently discovered practice of sex selective conception, invokes the right to life of women as a class, both in an immediate sense and as a right to perpetuation as a class, placing "reliance on equality and equal protection where the relevant issue involves systematic hierarchy and subordination".[39]

Law reform

In 1991, the CEDAW Committee found that

> . . . not all reports of States Parties adequately reflected the close connection between discrimination against women,

> gender-based violence, and violations of human rights and fundamental freedoms. The full implementation of the Convention requires States to take positive measures to eliminate all forms of violence against women.

Fixing responsibility on the state, the recommendation says that,

> States may also be responsible for private acts if they fail to act with due diligence to prevent violations of rights or to investigate and punish acts of violence, and for providing compensation.

Violence itself, in this recommendation, is defined very broadly to include acts that inflict physical, mental or sexual harm or suffering, threats of such acts, coercion and other deprivations of liberty.

Since 1995, women's groups have lobbied successfully to put together shadow reports on CEDAW that focus on different aspects of violence, in stark contrast to government reports, in the process taking the discussion on the Women's Convention to the grassroots. India's initial government report came up for consideration by the CEDAW Committee in 1999, and while it presented statistics pertaining to each article of CEDAW, there was no reference made at all to General Recommendation 19 on violence against women.

Commenting on the questions posed by the CEDAW Committee, the government of India representative said, "The questions asked were aggressive, but not hostile, probing but not inquisitorial. In our replies we emphasized . . . the fact that guarantees in our Constitution pre-date CEDAW and are not confined to discrimination against women alone." However, the concluding comments of the CEDAW Committee to the government report indicate quite clearly the influence of women's rights and human rights movements in the country, and in fact reflect their concerns. The government response and assertions predictably skirt critical issues of concern, justifying the status quo with easy recourse to platitudes about Constitutional provisions. However, in terms of standard-setting instruments for the treatment of women, even where these standards have already been set by national constitutions, both the CEDAW process and the office of the Special Rapporteur on Violence against Women are critical. This section will examine efforts at legislative reform in the areas discussed so far, and the interlinking of this reform with CEDAW and other conventions.

While we do see a slight shift in the judicial discourse on domestic violence in courts and an increased awareness of the magnitude of the problem, the direct impact of the CEDAW process is manifest in the passage of The Protection of Women from Domestic Violence Act, 2005 (No. 43 of 2005):

> An Act to provide for more effective protection of the rights of women, guaranteed under the Constitution, who are victims of violence of any kind occurring within the family and for matters connected therewith or incidental thereto; equality before the law and equal protection of the law . . .

and Article 21, which secures for them the right to life and personal liberty. Against this background of commitments to pro-active justice, domestic violence has operated as a severe form of oppression for women, thereby affecting their fundamental rights. It is therefore necessary and imperative to recognize the rights of women to protection against violence, and to residence in their shared household. Domestic violence has been defined in the legislation as an act, by omission or commission, or any conduct of the respondent which:

(*a*) harms or injures or endangers the health, safety, life, limb or well-being, whether mental or physical, of the aggrieved person or tends to do so, and includes physical abuse, sexual abuse, verbal and emotional abuse and economic abuse; or
(*b*) harasses, harms, injures or endangers the aggrieved person with a view to coerce her or any other person related to her to meet any unlawful demand for any dowry; or other property or valuable security; or
(*c*) the aggrieved person or any person related to her by any conduct mentioned in clauses (*a*) and (*b*); or
(*d*) otherwise injures or causes harm, whether physical or mental, to the aggrieved person.

The abuse that women face is multiple and simultaneous. One confounding feature of existing legislation like the Dowry Prohibition Act hinges on the definition of dowry, and the nexus between violence in the matrimonial home and transactions that fall within the meaning of dowry. The fact, however, is that violence in the matrimonial home is not confined to dowry demands, nor does it abate with the satisfaction of those demands. Keeping this in view, the term "abuse" has been defined in expansive rather than restrictive terms:

> *Physical abuse* includes any act or conduct which is of such a nature as to cause bodily pain, harm, or danger to life, limb or health, or impair the health or development of the person aggrieved and includes assault, criminal intimidation and criminal force.

Sexual abuse includes any conduct of a sexual nature that abuses, humiliates, degrades or otherwise violates the dignity.

Verbal and emotional abuse includes

(*a*) insults, ridicule, humiliation, name calling, specially with regard to not having a child or a male child; or
(*b*) repeated threats to cause physical pain to any person in whom the person aggrieved is interested.

Economic abuse includes

(*a*) deprivation of any or all economic or financial resources to which the person aggrieved is entitled under law or custom, whether payable under an order of court or otherwise, or which the person aggrieved requires out of necessity, including but not limited to household necessities for the person aggrieved and her children, if any; stridhan, property, jointly or separately owned by the persons aggrieved; payment of rental related to the shared household and maintenance;
(*b*) disposal of household effects, any alienation of assets whether movable or immovable, valuables, shares, securities, bonds, etc. or other property in which the person aggrieved has an interest or is entitled to use by virtue of the domestic relationship or which may be reasonably required by the person aggrieved or her children; or her stridhan or any other property jointly or separately held by the person aggrieved; or,
(*c*) prohibiting or restricting continued access to resources or facilities which the person aggrieved is entitled to use or enjoy by virtue of the domestic relationship, including access to the shared household.

A quick glance at reported cases on dowry-related violence demonstrates that reporting occurs only when violence has crossed the limits of endurance. Women do not report the first incidence of abuse, nor are they encouraged to do so either by their families or by officers of the criminal justice system. Rather they are counselled to return and "adjust" to the situation and, in general, be acquiescent in order for the violence to abate. Addressing the problem of grave assault, the proposed legislation states that "a single act of commission or omission may constitute domestic violence". However, the new legislation does pose a set of new problems with respect to the reconciliation of criminal and civil procedures.

A further point to note is the inclusion of the term "sexual abuse" within the meaning of abuse. This is when the Law Commission of India in its 172nd Report on the Review of Rape Laws in the year 2000, was unwilling to recommend an amendment that removed the exception to the definition of rape, arguing that including marital rape in it would constitute unnecessary interference in the institution of the family. The Domestic Violence Act cuts against that exception in Section 375 IPC by bringing sexual abuse within the meaning of rape. It is not clear, however, whether the provisions of the Act will override the Exception to Section 375 IPC because it speaks of sexual abuse, not explicitly of sexual assault or intercourse with a wife without her consent. Considering that the Criminal Law Amendment Act, 2006 does not remove the exception to the definition of rape, marital rape will continue to remain unaddressed by the criminal justice system, despite these legislative reforms.

One of the most serious problems faced by survivors of domestic violence is eviction from the matrimonial home. This is especially onerous when the abused woman's links with her natal family are tenuous. Women, in several cases even middle-aged women with adult children, face the grim prospect of destitution at the will of the husband. To offer specific protection against this, the Domestic Violence Act states that

> . . . every woman in a domestic relationship shall have the right to reside in the shared household, whether or not she has any right, title or beneficial interest in the same. An aggrieved woman shall have the right not to be evicted or excluded from the shared household or any part of it by the respondent save in accordance with the procedure established by law.

Being located in the matrimonial home after reporting spousal abuse logically increases the vulnerability of such women to graver assault, even loss of life. It is therefore not enough to offer women the right to reside in the shared household, there must be an additional protection against further abuse. Section 9 states that:

The court on being satisfied on a balance of probabilities that domestic violence has taken place, may pass a Protection Order prohibiting the respondent from:

(*i*) committing any act of domestic violence;
(*ii*) aiding and abetting in the commission of acts of domestic violence;
(*iii*) entering the place of employment of the person aggrieved or, if person aggrieved is a child, its school; or any other place frequented by the person aggrieved;

(*iv*) attempting to communicate in any form whatsoever with the person aggrieved, including personal, oral or written, electronic or telephonic contact;

(*v*) committing any other act as specified in the protection order;

(*vi*) alienating any assets, operating bank lockers or bank accounts used or held or enjoyed by both parties, jointly or singly by the respondent; including her stridhan or any other property held either jointly by the parties or separately by them;

(*vii*) causing violence to the dependents, other relatives and persons who give the person aggrieved assistance from domestic violence.

In addition the court, on being satisfied on a balance of probabilities, that domestic violence has taken place, may pass a Residence Order to restrain the respondent from dispossessing or in any manner disturbing the possession of the aggrieved person from the shared household; direct the respondent to remove himself from the shared household; restrain the respondent or any of his relatives from entering any portion of the shared household in which the aggrieved person resides; restrain the respondent from alienating or dispossessing the shared household or encumbering the same; restrain the respondent from renouncing his rights in the shared household except in favour of the person aggrieved; and/or direct the respondent to secure alternate accommodation for the person aggrieved or to pay rent for the same, if circumstances so require.

Under Section 10 the court may direct the respondent to pay monetary relief to meet the expenses incurred and losses suffered by the person aggrieved and any child, as a result of the domestic violence and includes, but is not limited to, loss of earnings, medical expenses, loss caused due to the destruction, damage or removal of any property from the control of the person aggrieved, maintenance for the person aggrieved as well as her children, if any, including an order under, or in addition to, an order under Section 125, CrPC, and compensation for the domestic violence inflicted upon the person aggrieved.

Apart from preventing the person accused of abuse from committing acts of violence, the new legislation introduces the principle of compensation for victim-survivors of abuse, for the first time. The impact of the CEDAW process on the issue of domestic violence in India is to be seen most directly in this effort of lawyers, civil society initiatives and policy makers to put in place legislation that will offer women protection against discrimination and abuse in the matrimonial home.

Conclusion

The reason for the persistence of discrimination is that there has been no fundamental transformation in the body politic or in the composition of institutions of governance. Ironically, the legislature and the judiciary are the two institutions which have been the most resistant to implementing the equality code of the Constitution with respect to gender and caste.

The government, through the legislature and with the active support of the executive, has been pro-active in enacting beneficial legislation in several areas—property rights, domestic violence, pre-natal and pre-conception sex selection—and policy-makers are increasingly alive to the complexity of gender-based discrimination. The judiciary has taken a radical view with respect to women's guardianship rights, sexual harassment at the workplace, sexual assault, communal sexual crimes and collective violence. However, the situation on the ground, while much better documented, does not demonstrate the positive impact of such governmental interest. The most critical problem lies in continuing resistance to equal representation for women in the legislature and judiciary—the law-making and law-enforcing institutions are among the most hostile in terms of discrimination against women, in their very constitution.

Notes & references

[1] Patricia Viseur Sellers, "Sexual Violence and Peremptory Norms: The Legal Value of Rape," 34 *Case Western Reserve Journal of International Law*, pp. 287–303, 2002.
[2] John Harris, *Violence and Responsibility* (London: Routledge and Kegan Paul, 1980).
[3] Upendra Baxi, "Twilight of Human Rights", Lecture, August, 2003.
[4] Cheris Kramarae in Karen A. Foss, Sonja K. Foss and Cindy L. Griffin (eds.), *Feminist Rhetorical Theories* (Thousand Oaks: Sage Publications, 1998).
[5] *Vishaka vs. State of Rajasthan* (1997) 6 SCC 241.
[6] The campaign around the case of Bhanwari Devi is of course much larger than the issue of sexual harassment at the workplace, and will be dealt with in a separate chapter.
[7] Padmini Swaminathan, "The Trauma of Wage Employment" in Kalpana Kannabiran (ed.), *The Violence of Normal Times*. op. cit.
[8] In 1987, Rupan Deol Bajaj, an IAS officer and K.P.S. Gill, an IPS officer were present with other colleagues at a dinner hosted by another government officer, when Gill, in full view of all present, assaulted Rupan Bajaj and spoke to her in a derogatory manner, leading her to register an FIR under Section 354 of the Indian Penal Code, "Outraging the Modesty of a Woman". The High Court of Punjab and Haryana quashed the FIR, using Section 95 IPC, which states "[n]othing is an offence by reason that it causes, or that it is intended to cause . . . any harm, if that harm is so slight that no person of ordinary sense and temper would complain of the harm". The Supreme Court reversed the High Court judgement in 1995 and convicted Gill. *Rupan Deol Bajaj vs. K.P.S. Gill*, (1995) 6 SCC 194.
[9] For a detailed discussion of this see Kalpana Kannabiran and Vasanth Kannabiran, "Outrageous Modesty, Outraged Honour," in *De-Eroticising Assault: Essays on Modesty, Honour and Power* (Calcutta: Stree, 2002).
[10] 1980-(SC2)-GJX -0165 -SC, *Krishan Lal, Petitioner vs. State of Haryana, Respondent.* Emphasis added. This statement is repeated in *Chandraprakash Kewalchand Jain* (1990), *Gurmit Singh* (1996) *and State of HP vs. Lekh Raj and Another* (1999).

[11] *Vishaka vs. State of Rajasthan* (1997) 6 SCC 241.
[12] *Vishaka vs. State of Rajasthan*, Supreme Court of India, Criminal Original Jurisdiction, Writ Petition (Criminal)Nos. 666–70 of 1992.
[13] Ibid.
[14] For a comprehensive review of case law and debates, see Vicki Schultz, "Reconceptualizing Sexual Harassment," *The Yale Law Journal*, 107:6, April 1998, pp. 1683–1805.
[15] The Code of Good Practice on the Handling of Sexual Harassment Cases, 1998, significantly under the Labour Relations Act, 1995 in South Africa, is an example of good practice.
[16] For a detailed discussion on the relevance of the classification-discrimination arguments to feminist jurisprudence on equality, see Kalpana Kannabiran, "Towards a Jurisprudence of Women's Rights in India", Alladi Krishnaswami Memorial Lecture, Hyderabad, October 2, 2003.
[17] *M.I. Shahdad vs. Mohd. Abdullah Mir and Others*, AIR 1967 Jammu & Kashmir 120
[18] *J.R. Clement Regis vs. State of Tamil Nadu*. 1993 II CLR 651.
[19] *Lt. (Mrs.) Indira Kumari Kartiayoni vs. The Maha Nideshak, Raksha Mantralaya, Shastra Sena Chikitsa Seva, New Delhi, & Others.* AIR 1991 SC 416.
[20] *Radha Charan Patnaik vs. State of Orissa and Another*, AIR 1969 Orissa 237 (V56 C84). The Indian Administrative Service (Recruitment) Rules, 1954, excluded married women from posts included in that service on the ground that *marriage brings about certain disabilities and obligations* which may affect the efficiency or suitability of employment.
[21] Justice Krishna Iyer in *C.B. Muthamma vs. Union of India*, AIR 1979 SC 1868.
[22] Vicki Schultz, "Reconceptualizing Sexual Harassment," op.cit.
[23] AIR 1972 Punjab and Haryana 117. Emphasis added.
[24] *J.R. Clement Regis vs. State of Tamil Nadu*.
[25] *Lt. (Mrs.) Indira Kumari Kartiayoni vs. The Maha Nideshak*, etc.
[26] *Air India vs. Nergesh Meerza & Others* AIR 1981 SC 1829 and *Air India Cabin Crew Association vs. Yeshaswinee Merchant & Others* AIR 2004 SC 187.

[27] Martha Minow, *Making all the Difference: Inclusion and Exclusion in American Law* (Ithaca: Cornell University Press, 1990).
[28] Draft Article 42 of the Indian Constitution which was dropped without a debate. B. Shiva Rao, *The Framing of India's Constitution.*
[29] Values of western women should not be applied to Indian women, said Justice Thakker in *Bharwada Bhoginbhai Hirjibhai,* because Indian women even experienced rape differently from western women.
[30] See especially, Muvalur Ramamirthammal's *Web of Deceit: Devadasi Reform in Colonial India* edited and translated by Kalpana Kannabiran and Vasanth Kannabiran (New Delhi: Kali for Women, 2003).
[31] *T. Sareetha vs. T. Venkatasubbaiah,* AIR 1983 Andhra Pradesh 356.
[32] 172nd Report of the Law Commission on Review of Rape Laws.
[33] *Saritha vs. R. Ramachandra,* 2002 (4) ALT 592 (D.B.)
[34] The inevitability points to the logical consequences of particular structures.
[35] A.R. Nanda, "National Population Policy: Small Family Norm and Sex Selection," Paper presented at the Seminar on "The New Paradigm of Development and Sex Selection", New Delhi, August 2004.
[36] AIR 2003 SC 3309.
[37] *Malpani Infertility Clinic Pvt. Ltd. and Ors. vs. Appropriate Authority, PNDT Act and Ors.* AIR 2005 Bom 26.
[38] Ronald Dworkin, *Freedom's Law: The Moral Reading of the American Constitution* (Cambridge: Harvard University Press, 1996).
[39] Martha C. Nussbaum, "Sex Equality, Liberty, and Privacy: A Comparative Approach to the Feminist Critique." In Zoya Hasan, E. Sridharan and R. Sudarshan (eds.), *India's Living Constitution: Ideas, Practices, Controversies* (Delhi: Permanent Black, 2004), p. 273.

3 Alternative Forms of Protest

Ritu Menon

THE 1990s marked something of an unusual departure for the Indian women's movement as far as campaigning on issues was concerned. For one, terms and strategies like "advocacy" and "lobbying" began to be used much more commonly than before; parliamentarians and pressure groups were sought out to hear representations and field questions in Parliament; women's groups engaged in discussions and organized campaigns with national and state commissions on women on several issues, ranging from sex work to child abuse and the impact of globalization on women; and any number of "gender sensitisation" trainings were carried out with the judiciary, the police, bureaucrats, probationers in the central administrative and foreign services, and so on. Underlying these efforts and activities was the implicit—and sometimes explicit—acknowledgement that a purposive interaction with institutional machinery and systems was critical in influencing positive outcomes for women; specifically for incorporating a gender perspective into the policy and planning process. In one sense, this "mainstreaming" of women's issues marked an important break from the protest activism of the late 1970s and 1980s, when street demonstrations, demands for legal reform, and more direct confrontations with the state were much more in evidence. Other chapters in this book discuss the relative success or failure of feminist interventions on the issue of violence against women, especially with regard to legal reform, changes in policy, a recognition of sexual harassment at the workplace, post the Bhanwari Devi rape case, and a reformulation of guidelines regarding the same. In this chapter we discuss three campaigns or initiatives on violence against women by the women's movement—now much more broadly defined to include groups and organizations that may not have women's issues as their primary focus, but centrally address the question of violence against women in the context of ethnic violence and militarism. The three campaigns are notable not only because they are so different in scope and articulation, but because they indicate an evolution in the way violence against women has been perceived and conceptualized over the last twenty-five years.

I

"Back on Track!": The Railway Campaign

On March 8, 1998, women's organizations in Delhi launched what is called the Railway Campaign, demanding "safer travelling conditions for women and reclaiming our right to travel safely in public transport without the threat, fear or experience of sexual violence."[1] The impetus for the campaign was the consequence of a personal experience of violence in a train on January 1, 1998. A group of 10 women were travelling on the Tata-Muri Express from Ranchi (Bihar) to Delhi after attending the Sixth National Conference of Women's Movements in India. In their words, during the journey

> . . . three army jawans, who consumed alcohol throughout the thirty-hour journey, sang rude songs, directed lewd stares, called out names and obstructed our paths as we

> passed by. Upon arriving at New Delhi Railway Station, one of the last women to get off the train was physically assaulted by one of the drunk men. When she retaliated by slapping him, he shouted obscenities and hit her. Although we immediately located a RPF (Railway Protection Force) person, he was of no help and let the offenders go without even asking for their identification. It took ten of us four hours to file an FIR after this and ensure that the culprits be traced! The case, registered with the NHRC (National Human Rights Commission) and in civil courts, then taken over by the Army's Court of Inquiry, has still not been concluded.[2]

Predictably, the railway authorities dragged their feet when the women complained and their attitude, especially that of the Government Railway Police (GRP), was dismissive and patronising. The Railway Protection Force went so far as to say, "We take care of property, not people." Incensed by this response, but no longer silent, women decided that this time they would take their protest beyond street demonstrations, onto the railway tracks themselves. On March 8, therefore, International Women's Day, over 60 women dressed in black hit New Delhi Railway Station and spent eight hours there, putting up thousands of posters and distributing more than 5,000 pamphlets on platforms and trains. The Railway Union, through the Hind Mazdoor Sabha, actively supported the campaign and, for the first time, announcements regarding the sexual harassment of women on trains were made on the public address system.

Between April and July 1998, this protest was carried out every month at different railway stations, and at different times, covering day and night trains to different destinations. In addition to pamphleteering, plays were performed, songs sung and slogans raised. In Rajasthan, the women's wing of the Western Railways Employees' Union (Kota) and the South Eastern Railways Employees' Union (Vishakhapatnam) carried out similar campaigns in their regions. Women in Calcutta, under the banner of the organization, Maitrayee, took up the case of a Bangladeshi woman who was raped in the Howrah Yatri Niwas at Howrah Station. (The case was finally won and the woman awarded Rs. 10 lakhs as compensation.)[3]

From July to September 1998, the campaign was sustained and extended to raising public awareness on the issue through the media, and representations to the Railway Minister. Television programmes with prominent anchors called, "Chalti ka Naam Gaadi" highlighted sexual violence in the railways, and a petition was filed by Jagori, a women's resource centre, which spearheaded the campaign against the army. The case was finally heard—in army courts—but only after pressure was brought to bear on them by the National Human Rights Commission.

The basic issues that the campaign wished to highlight were

- Reclaim women's right to free movement: to go anywhere at any time, free from the fear of harassment/violence/abuse.
- De-trivialise assault: Most people, including the woman herself, feel that lewd stares, songs, words and threats are not 'as bad' as rape. As the reactions of co-passengers and police highlight, there is a hierarchy of violence where some offences are more acceptable and treated as 'normal'. This is a fallacy that ignores what a woman faces

every time she leaves the house, bracing herself for abuse. Every woman has the right to safe travel and bodily integrity. No violation is acceptable.

- Give direct visibility to the issue and break the silence that surrounds such crimes: Women maintain that it is not 'their fault' that such crimes occur. Often we are made to feel ashamed, and therefore try to maintain silence when we do face abuse. We are blamed by authorities, perpetrators and public alike for, say, our clothes, daring to go out at night, travelling on a train alone, and so on. By realizing that this stigma is constructed, and by speaking out against it, we can identify the attitudes that victimize us and map out strategies to combat them. Only through highlighting the occurrence of the phenomenon will the appropriate authorities take responsibility and act.
- Support women who file complaints and speak out against such crimes: The truth is that it is difficult to speak out against sexual harassment if there is no support from the public, and especially from family members or those close to us. It is a vicious circle. The onus to seek justice cannot be only on the woman. It is critical that family members and members of the public recognize that sexual violence is a crime and is not the result of a woman's behaviour, her appearance, etc.

In April 1999, one year after the Campaign was launched, the Railway Board issued an important order, Standing Order No. 57, directing RPF officials to prevent crimes against women.[4] In April 2001, the NHRC convened a meeting (based on Jagori's petition) between Jagori members, railway ministry officials, and the RPF; and in February 2002, four years later, the NHRC issued landmark directives to the Railway Ministry to take action to protect the rights of women travelling in trains. The directions explicitly asked the railways to:

- Ensure that FIR forms are easily available on trains in all languages relevant to the routes concerned.
- Disseminate information as to who women passengers should approach and lodge a complaint with.
- Ensure that people are provided with complete information about the procedure to be followed in filling out FIRs in running trains
- Come up with appropriate notices at strategic points in all railway stations/coaches highlighting that sexual assaults, obscene remarks and all kinds of unwanted attention are forms of sexual harassment punishable under the Indian Penal Code and Railways Act.[5]

II

Although the Railway Campaign displayed some of the familiar features of earlier campaigns, such as sloganeering, leafleteering and demonstrating, it differed from them in other noteworthy ways. Unlike Women in Black, for instance, another remarkable campaign sustained over a long period of time, the Railway Campaign was much more than a symbolic protest. Where Women in Black continue to meet once a week and stage a silent protest in a busy public place, the Railway Campaign extended over five years in a concerted attempt at action every month for the first year, focussing on unsafe travel on Indian trains. Where Women in Black relies on a single repeated gesture, the power of silent indictment and the dramatic visual impact of being dressed in black, the colour of mourning, the Railway

Campaign used a multipronged strategy: making representations to concerned departments and ministries; demonstrating every month at different railway stations; filing a case against the army; petitioning the NHRC; drawing attention to the issue of unsafe travel on national broadcast and print media; and bringing sustained pressure to bear on the Railway Ministry, resulting in the standing order of March 1999, and the NHRC directive to the Railway Ministry of 2002.

The interaction by the women's movement with these various agencies of the government departed from earlier practice in one important respect: it was an active, positive engagement rather than a purely adversarial one, inviting ministers and the bureaucracy to participate in ensuring safer travel, while *at the same time* insisting on accountability through seeking the intervention of the NHRC and the courts. For the first time, too, the Railway Campaign forged alliances with trade unions within the railways, thus expanding the scope as well as the representation of the protest. This also meant that the action was physically and geographically dispersed across the country, adding to the slow buildup of pressure on the railways to respond. Of much greater significance than all this, however, is the fact that trade unions, also for the first time, allied with the women's movement on the issue of violence against women, taking it on board as a labour issue, as well.

Equally significant, at another level, is the fact that the Railway Campaign sought out the NHRC rather than the National Commission for Women (NCW) for redress, even though cases of violence against women fall expressly within the latter's purview and are its particular charge. This tactical shift, we suggest, was prompted by earlier experiences with the NCW—perhaps most notably in the Bhanwari Devi rape case of the mid-1990s—and the recognition that the NCW is not empowered to act on its own. Although it may, *suo motu,* take up a case and conduct its own investigation into it, its findings can only be submitted to the Home Ministry and the Law Commission for action; at most, it may recommend remedies or further enquiry, but it cannot issue directives. In this regard the Railway Campaign was much more effectively served by the NHRC.

III

The Government of India apart, the Indian Railways are the largest employer in the country, and of the 13,000,000 passengers that its 7,000 passenger trains carry every day, a good percentage are women. The railways employees' unions, similarly, are among the largest national trade unions and, till recently, the more militant. To take a campaign on violence against women into the heart of this citadel, then, was something of a first for the women's movement, and a more detailed discussion of it therefore might be in order.

Breaching the barriers, both visible and invisible, presented the first challenge. As is well known, institutional structures, bureaucracies and law enforcement agencies are skilled in insulating themselves against public action at practically every level; thus, the women who tried to file an FIR against their assailants met with the kind of resistance we are all too familiar with. Not only are mechanisms for redressal almost defunct, but officials and police on trains and platforms are unresponsive and, occasionally, guilty of perpetrating such offences themselves. Railway stations rarely indicate the location of police patrollers, themselves inadequate and randomly placed. Further up the bureaucratic ladder, the inclination to pass the buck is almost irresistable; and as far as the armed forces are concerned, the tendency to deny culpability is almost axiomatic. More instructive, perhaps, and even unexpected, were the invisible barriers that women's groups encountered when they launched the Railway Campaign. As they put it in their report, all of them faced tremendous resistance in getting women at the stations to take the pamphlets being offered to them.[6]

Women were hesitant. They either plain refused, or displayed extreme diffidence; often, if they were with a male person they would look at them for permission, feeling that information being offered to them directly rather than to their husbands/ brothers/ fathers was not "right". Most men, meanwhile, felt it was their right to have this information; they thus came up to the activists and demanded that they be given the pamphlets. Others told the groups that they were wasting their time giving information to women. Some of them even refused to let them give the pamphlets to the women accompanying them.

On other occasions, the activists found that they were the only women in compartments occupied entirely by male passengers, subjected to lewd comments, hostile glances and active resistance to their attempts to engage them in discussion. These experiences underlined once again, just how male and aggressive our public spaces can be for women, and how and why their mobility is so constrained. Indeed, some spaces are so hostile that they almost allow, or at least enable, actual violence against women to take place, at the same time that the "protective" arms of government seem to condone it through silence or inaction. Subliminally, they appear to endorse the view that women should expect violence if they venture out of the private domain into the public. In the Railway Campaign this was borne out by the fact that repeated attempts by women's groups to meet the authorities, the railway minister and the Safety Review Committee were stonewalled.

Institutional barriers were crossed when, eight months after the Campaign was launched, women's groups sought the mediation of two other institutions that we might characterize as watchdog—the NHRC, and mainstream print and electronic media. In August 1998 *New Delhi Times* carried a report on the Railway Campaign, following which women were invited to participate in a popular prime time television programme, the Priya Tendulkar Show, on Star Plus. Four women's groups—Jagori, Action India, Sabla Sangh and the YWCA—participated in the programme called "Chalti ka Naam Gaadi", along with other individuals and the then Minister of State for Railways, Ram Naik, who had hitherto been inaccessible to the women. For the first time, there was a public, televised airing of the issue of safe travel for women on trains, and sexual violence, rather than derailment or stolen baggage, was discussed. This was not enough, however, and it was only towards the middle of 2001, two and a half years later, following an expose in *Outlook*[7] that the NHRC acted on the petition filed by Jagori. Two officials from the recalcitrant Railway Ministry and the Railway Protection Force met with members of Jagori, and a new round of negotiations began. In defence of the railways, however, it must

रेल मंत्रालय (रेलवे बोर्ड)
GOVERNMENT OF INDIA
MINISTRY OF RAILWAYS
(RAILWAY BOARD)

No.98/Sec(Cr.)/45/94 New Delhi,dated 08-3-99

The Chief Security Commissioners/RPF,
Northern Railway, New Delhi.

STANDING ORDER No.57

Sub: Crime against women passengers-role of RPF-regarding.

One of the important objectives before RPF is to promote passenger safety and security as defind in our mission statement. Needless to emphasise that anti-social elements cause a lot of inconvenience to the travelling public especially women passengers. Besides causing inconvenience to lady passengers it leads to loss of reputation to the Indian Railways. Authorities like GRP, Railway Commercial and RPF are required to prevent the incidents of crime against women passengers.

In a recent case, some miscreants threw chilli powder on the face of a lady commuter while she was travelling in a Ist Class compartment of a local train. Police had registered a case and has taken up investigation. In preventing such types of offences against the women passengers,RPF can play an important role. Under the Railway Act, 1989, RPF as a Railway servant have adequate powers to deal with such offenders. Section 179 of Railways Act, 1989 empowers RPF to arrest offenders withourt a warrant and further to produce before the nearest Magistrate. The action by the RPF may go a long way in curbing the menace.

For tackling the nuisance in an effective manner the section and the trains affected should be identified. A joint team of officers from Railway Commercial, RPF and GRP should be constituted which should conduct regular drives.

The vulnerable suburban sections should be identified. Ladies compartment of EMUs may be escorted by women constables. The drive may be launched at vulnerable stations.

RPF personnel should be sensitised,so as to understand the problems faced by women passengers. They should be trained to react effectively to situations where crime takes place against the women passengers.

Hindi version of Standing Order will follow. The Standing Order should be got translated to the regional languages and supplied to the Posts to display on the Notice Boards. The RPF peronnel should also be briefed on the contents of this SO.

(H.RAO)
Director General/RPF
Railway Board

be reiterated that the Railway Board had already issued its Standing Order 57 on Crime Against Women Passengers in March 1999.

IV

How is one to gauge the "success" or otherwise of the Railway Campaign? Can it really be considered "alternative"? No definitive or unambiguous response is possible, but if we might be permitted the analogy, we could say that it was an example of the two steps forward, one step back syndrome.

At the formal and judicial levels, the campaign met with qualified success. The army court let the three jawans off with a nominal fine and demotion. This might have been unsatisfactory and insufficient as far as women's groups and activists are concerned, but a demotion in the army is fairly strict punishment and counts as a seriously adverse career setback. The Railway Protection Force, on the other hand, got off extremely lightly because "the allegations against them could not be substantiated". Despite this, however, the Railway Board did issue its Standing Order on Crimes Against Women Passengers; it may be useful to reproduce the full text of the notification here because, in a sense, it exemplifies the ambivalence of the relationship between the women's movement and the government.

Using the language of the colonial state and subsequently that of successive penal codes, the order characterizes straightforward assaulters as "anti–social elements" and "miscreants". In the same way that legal language often uses the designations "psycopath", "deviant" or "pervert" to characterize rapists and child abusers, the Standing Order, too, individualises the offence by particularising it; it thereby deflects attention away from the general, and far more pervasive, problem of insecure travel for women and the failure of the RPF and GRP to ensure their safety. Given that the Railways Act (1989) empowers the RPF to arrest offenders without warrant its laxity in the majority of cases is inexcusable.

The entrenched attitude that women are a "vulnerable" section of the travelling public, in need of "protection", finds its echo in the provision regarding the escort of Ladies Compartments by women constables, and the suggestion that RPF personnel be "sensitized to understand the problems faced by women passengers". The whole is then muffled by the bland tone of the order, indicating perhaps, the kind of ennui induced in the bureaucracy if you insist that they take note of sexual harassment. Since the primary responsibility of the Railway Police Force is the protection of the travelling public and the safety of trains, passengers and the railways, one might ask why they need to "be trained to react effectively to situations where crimes take place against women passengers". The passive voice of the order, it would appear, suggests much more the aggrieved party than the aggressor.

By contrast, the tone of the NHRC directive to the Railway Ministry is pro-active and firm, clearly enunciating the rights of passengers, the rules and obligations of the Railway Ministry, and the responsibilities of the RPF. Leaving nothing to chance and no room for ambiguity, it directs the railways to actually and particularly ensure the safe travel of passengers by putting in place the mechanisms and means by which it is made possible. Making FIR forms available on all trains, in all languages, is a significant first step in encouraging complaints to be lodged, as well as an enabling mechanism for doing so. So, too, the dissemination of information regarding whom to contact when offences are committed, since most travellers are ignorant of this. Most important is the directive regarding filling out an FIR in a moving train since there is no police station on board; and, as is well known, most FIRs are rendered invalid because they have not been correctly filed. In short, where the Railway Board's self-definition is paternalistic and protective, the NHRC's directives insist that it fulfil its duties towards passengers by delivering justice.

The success of the Railway Campaign in gaining the support first, of the railway employees' unions and then the Railway Board, is significant in the context of the general resistance of institutions to charges of discrimination against women and gender inequality. On the volatile and vexed issue of violence against women, institutional resistance is compounded by cultural attitudes and patriarchal or male chauvinist rationalizations, often couched in the idiom of protection. Such attitudes permeate official responses and practices at all levels, and in time, crystallise to form what Naila Kabeer calls "the institutionalised construction of gender relations",[8] and hence the justification for gender inequality. By persuading the trade unions and petitioning the NHRC, the Campaign was successful in getting both institutions to take that initial step towards regarding violence against women as a labour issue in the first instance, and a social and political issue in the second. It also squarely placed this understanding in the discourse of rights rather than the vocabulary of welfare.

As with the state, the relationship of the women's movement with that other institution, mainstream media, has also been ambivalent, and over the years it has had to come to terms with both its power and its sexism. The struggle for space within it, as well as for a fair and positive representation by it have been discussed and analysed in detail by feminists, so a reiteration of their critique may not be necessary here. Latterly, however, and especially over the last 20 years, with the expansion of international electronic media, both the power and the inherent sexism of the mainstream have been vastly enhanced and intensified. The commodification of women is routine fare, glamourised to make it palatable, even desirable.

Yet, perhaps the first move made by many women's groups today when planning or launching action on an issue, is to hold a press conference, prepare press releases and otherwise solicit media time and space for their protest. In the Railway Campaign, the impact of coverage by the print media—*Outlook, New Delhi Times, Times of India*, etc.—and television—NDTV—cannot be discounted. Media attention can often be subversive, reinscribing the very stereotypes that are being challenged; that this did not happen in this case might be fortuitous, or it might be that media coverage came after three years of campaigning and awareness–raising; or it could be that a campaign directed at the country's largest employer and its transport lifeline merited more serious consideration.

But a campaign can only accomplish so much. On April 29, 2005, a railway police constable in Mumbai was arrested for assaulting and abusing women commuters on a local train. Simon Koli, posted in a ladies compartment, was booked for slapping a two months pregnant woman, aged 25. Several commuters also accused him of being drunk on duty. Two weeks prior to this incident, another railway constable misbehaved with a 24 year old woman at the Matunga Road Station, also using foul language. Meanwhile, female police officials have begun complaining about lewd remarks and sexual harrassment by male colleagues.[9]

Constable Koli has been charged under Sections 509 (threats), 354 (indecent behavior), 506 and 504 (verbal abuse); and 323 (assault) of the Indian Penal Code. If the Railway Campaign contributed in even a limited way to this outcome, it will have achieved part of its objective.

War & Peace: Ideology and the Architecture of Performance*

I

The possibility of using traditional ballet as an instrument of feminist activism and intervention arose for Asmita, a women's resource centre in Hyderabad, in January 2000. Four years later, the organization felt the need to take that initiative further by producing a second ballet, which explored in greater depth not just the issue of violence but also the grammar of Kuchipudi.

Aware of the significance of culture in gendering society, Asmita reflected on the need to penetrate traditional forms and subvert the culture and norms perpetrated by tradition, through fresh interpretations and perspectives. The role of religious myths in reinforcing and legitimizing patriarchal norms is critical, but has generally been difficult to contend with. The interpretation of these myths through traditional art forms, especially music and dance, carries a powerful effect that works at subliminal levels. It is as if classical music and dance are trapped in a patriarchal idiom from which they cannot be liberated. Several attempts have been made to use traditional forms to subvert patriarchal agendas from a women's perspective. Given the fact that the gendering of ordinary citizens and the shaping of their identities is derived largely from social norms, strengthened by figures and stories from traditional mythology, the group felt that the reinterpretation of mythological characters, especially women, and a radical re-reading of the significance of their actions might be useful.

* Excerpted from a longer version by Volga, Vasanth Kannabiran, A. Kutumba Rao & Kalpana Kannabiran.

Conflict, war and women

Work on conflict in the past two decades has looked at the specific implications of conflict for women. The organization of mothers' fronts; mobilizations by women to promote peace and resist war; the ways in which family and community lock women into inescapable custody through non-consensual marriage, widowhood and remarriage practices; the experiences of combatant women within militant movements and resistance struggles; the relationship between the violent masculinity of the armed forces and women at contested boundaries or on the borders of nations, are all areas that have been explored in depth in feminist writing on conflict, especially on the subcontinent. The starkness of the violence of war has often been most powerfully expressed through the performative mode; Asmita zeroed in on Kuchipudi, and dance, as their chosen medium, in part because of the heavy reliance that Kuchipudi places on the interpretation of mythic traditions, especially the two epics, *Ramayana* and *Mahabharata*.

The centre-piece of the *Ramayana* is the abduction of Sita by Ravana, king of Sri Lanka, and the battle for her recovery by her husband, Rama, and his army. The subversion in the ballet produced by Asmita lay in its turning the spotlight on Sita as protagonist, articulating her situation.

Nay, not for me the weight of that crown!
Not for me the burden of that identity!

And what is the weight or the burden that Sita speaks about?

Sita, bereft of peace by Rama's lust for power
Sita, of sorrow appropriated by Ravana
Sita, consummating my purity in the flames
To prove my virtue to a husband
Swollen with the pride of victory.

Abduction is not unfamiliar to us. The history of Partition, especially of the Punjab, echoes this experience of abduction, recovery and rejection, so that Sita comments not on the glorious battle but reflects instead on the eerie timelessness of her experience. Abduction is not a story of one side of the border alone, and it is often countered by deceit, appropriation and the assault of women by the other side. Again, Surpanaka is central to the telling of the story of Rama's exile; yet the epics speak not of her violation, but of Rama's valour. It is this emphasis that has found expression in traditional classical dance. Narratives of Partition in the subcontinent led Asmita to exploring alternative interpretations of the figure of Surpanaka in the *Ramayana*, giving her a voice on par with Sita's. For those who have always thought of Surpanaka "as the Dravida maid/Celebrating beauty, worshipping nature . . . Woman of the universe [who] pour[s] forth love/Transcending barriers of caste and creed . . . Despised, reviled for desiring love/Punished, mutilated for craving love/Surpanaka a flaming torch/Living testimony to untold violation and shame", there was the sudden realization that a radically different interpretation can indeed be based on a history of the present.

The section of "War & Peace" that dealt with the *Ramayana* ended with Sita and Surpanaka speaking together, as allies, of the untold violation of women in the war between the Aryas and the Dravidas. The insertion of the critical element in feminist politics, the need for women to build alliances across borders, boundaries and identities, even while acknowledging the fact of diversity, through the figures of Sita and Surpanaka had a dramatic effect on the audience. In suggesting this, the group was in fact drawing on the letter written by Pakistani women to the women of Bangladesh, apologizing for the violence perpetrated by the Pakistani army during the 1971 Bangladeshi war of independence.

In the *Mahabharata*, Draupadi introduces the experience of disrobing and the public humiliation of women—an experience that women's movements have had to confront time and again. For Madhavi, daughter of King Yayati, who was gifted by her father to the sage Galava, the fulfillment of her father's obligation to the sage meant being left with one king after another, in succession, to bear them sons so that the sage could collect the thousand white horses he desired in return. Forced pregnancies, the rape of Bangladeshi women and the experience of ethnic cleansing in the former Yugoslavia compelled a re-examination of the "mythic" nature of this myth. Was this myth or was it, in fact, the story of patriarchy?

Ever since the ballet was first performed in 2000, "War & Peace" has been taken to every district in Andhra Pradesh and has completed 50 performances in six years, each performance being witnessed by an audience of 600 to 1,000 people. Some time in 2004, the group began to feel the need to address other issues, especially that of domestic violence. The Andhra Pradesh state legislature had begun to roll back the gains of the women's movement by making Section 498 A of the IPC compoundable. The rhetoric in courts and police stations shifted to speaking about the "treachery" of women in filing cases against "unsuspecting" husbands. Meanwhile women continued to suffer grave assault, often leading to death within the matrimonial home. On March 8, 2004, a second play, "Lakshmana Rekha" was presented to an audience of *five thousand predominantly poor rural women* from different districts in Andhra Pradesh, after a public hearing on violence against women.

The dance began by celebrating pioneering women like Jotiba and Savitribai Phule, Durgabai Deshmukh, Chityala Ailamma, Suvarthamma of Karamchedu, the women of Chundur, and activists in the anti-arrack movement. In replacing goddesses with Dalit women and women's rights activists and introducing them through their struggles, the ballet marked a radical shift in reorienting viewers.

The lakshmana rekha—an echo from the *Ramayana*, in which Rama's brother Lakshmana draws a line on the ground beyond which Sita cannot venture—divides the public from the private, ensuring the protection of women who live within private spaces in patriarchies and conform to the codes of domesticity. What would the actions of these iconised and idealised women have looked like when bereft of the glow of sacrifice? Gandhari, who blindfolded herself on her marriage to the blind King Dhritarashtra, has traditionally been seen as the ideal wife and companion. Given the widespread occurrence of forced, non-consensual marriages and the abuse that women face in these subservient relationships, Gandhari's act can be seen as one of powerful resistance.

This is my vengeance
My raging anguish
My eyes shall not gaze upon a husband
I do not choose
No companion will I be
To a man I do not love
No service or shoulder will I offer
To a lord forced upon me.

Urmila, Lakshmana's wife, is left behind while Lakshmana follows his duty to be with his brother, Rama, at all times. She goes into a deep slumber that lasts for fourteen years.

Within my eyes a fathomless ocean
of anger and bitter sorrow
An unvoiced war cry resounds in my heart
Rejecting my wifely duties
Slumber is the weapon of my satyagraha.

For Renuka, wife of sage Jamadagni and mother of Parasurama, a fleeting moment of desire results in death, and the gift of life is a gift from father to son.

What is the price of chastity?
What is the power of motherhood?
Should the heart not falter even for a moment?
This then is the price of chastity
This then is the power of motherhood
For a life restored in charity
Where is the desire to live
Or the heart to serve?
Chastity is but a pot of sand
Motherhood but a magic deer

What price these thrones empty of authority or meaning?

"War & Peace" and "Lakshmana Rekha," productions of 75 minutes each with lyrics set to music and pre-recorded, have made extensive use of contemporary feminist research and texts to draw connections between myth and the violence of war in our day. The specific works that Asmita drew upon were recent feminist writing on the experiences of women during the partition of India; Sri Lankan women's war poetry; the violence against women of Bangladesh during their war of independence; and reports from the Vienna Tribunal and other writing on ethnic cleansing in the former Yugoslavia. Apart from introducing contemporary political themes into traditional classical dance, the ballets fundamentally interrogate the construction of gender, ideology and hegemony in the theory of dance itself, and especially of Kuchipudi. While an exhaustive analysis of this aspect may not be possible here, a few critical aspects of the performative traditions of dance may be worth discussing.

The *bhakti* (devotional) and *srungara* (desirable) *rasas* (essences) are important not just to representational forms but to an understanding of lived experience as well. To that extent, all *rasas* bridge the distance between performance and life. However, it is precisely through an unravelling of this connection that the patriarchal underpinnings of this theory are uncovered. It is a fact that women performers and *bhaktins* have, time and again, subverted hegemonic structures and resisted them; yet, the performative and material contexts of *rasa* have remained confined in the frameworks of dominance, notwithstanding shifts within those frameworks, and women performers have generally expressed either *bhakti* or *srungara,* devotion or desirability.

Domains of agency and expression are most evident in the language used to describe the *nayaka* ("ever victorious", "warrior without peer", "glorious emperor", "vanquisher of valorous kings") and the *nayika* (compliant consort, petulant or pining lover), especially in terms of figures of speech and moods. For the *nayika,* the most appropriate states are absolute surrender, sorrow, grief, love—depicted through stillness, laughing or smiling. In this context women are the *ashtama bhoga*—subject/objects, not agents/creators/protectors, with the power to give or take life. Apart from words, there is a hierarchy of language as well, with men of the upper castes speaking Sanskrit and women and shudras speaking Prakrit. Gender therefore suffuses the vocabulary of dance in unspoken, unquestioned and pervasive ways.

In this context, both "War and Peace" and "Lakshmana Rekha" peel off different layers of this encrustation in radical ways. The woman is no longer consort, sister, wife, mother; nor is she a willing, unquestioning subject who allows the reification of her subservience. The moment the woman is transformed into active agent/creator, pathos is replaced by resistance, the static smile with anger. In questioning the fundamentals of patriarchal subjugation on stage, the *rasa* travels from performance to lived experience, forcing self-reflection on the dancer.

Moving from a hegemonic binary portrayal of good and evil to a portrayal of diversity, equally positioned and equally valued, entails learning a different grammer of representation, one that does not exist within the pedagogy of Kuchipudi as it is taught today. Surpanaka need not be portrayed as grotesque, lacking in grace, heavy on her feet, a caricature of unwomanliness; this was something the dancers in "War & Peace" understood only gradually—that Surpanaka, like Sita, can also be portrayed as a graceful woman.

Finally, as far as dance tradition is concerned, the *Dasavatara* is a very typical presentation in Kuchipudi—the *laya*, the *raga* and the method convey the essence of the dance form. For scholars of Kuchipudi, tampering with the *Dasavatara* is unimagineable; but if in fact one is thinking in terms of incarnations, and of re-inscribing a woman's place in the body politic, what better way than to present the various incarnations of women? With a minor alteration in metre—purely precautionary—we presented the *Dasavatara* of aspirations as the culmination of "Lakshmana Rekha", as the only possible resolution to its boundaries:

I aspire to
Cross the frontiers of learning
To excel in games of speed and skill
To soar into space, exploring
Search and research the paths of science
To reach unimagined heights
  of glory in music and dance
To paint the world richly
Sculpt the human form to perfection
To lead struggles to victory.

In its early history Kuchipudi was a dance form that excluded women completely. The fact that it had never used the interpretations introduced before meant that dancers had to draw upon their repertoire very differently. In contemporary Kuchipudi, collective performances with several dancers of equal stature and experience are practically unknown, the individual always being centre-stage. Asmita's requirement of collective performance brought about a radical shift in dynamics between dancers, and meant that each dancer had to focus not just on her part but on the whole. Notions of collectivity and sharing thus entered a very different arena.

The public reaction to the ballets has been predictable. Viewers accustomed to relaxing to the melody of traditional music and graceful movements found that they had imperceptibly entered a world of violence, greed and horror. The reality of that world, seldom depicted on stage through this medium, has had a startling impact on middle class audiences; and the subversion of traditional legends and characters has been dramatic in its effect.

"Shed No More Blood": Naga Mothers' Association

I

> "When the Indian army came, it was the women who stepped forward between the villagers and the soldiers, it is only women who can intervene. We constantly had to talk to the army. We mothers would go to the warring factions, walk to their camps and plead with them not to kill each other and not to harass the villagers. We mothers can't stay quiet."
>
> —*Jotsoma village women*

Twenty-odd years ago, in February 1984, the Naga Mothers' Association (NMA) was founded in Kohima, the capital of Nagaland, as a voluntary organization open to all Naga women. It was formed in response to more than three decades of violence, armed conflict and social upheaval in Nagaland, intended to be a forum where issues of concern to Naga women, in particular, and Naga society in general could be raised. Although its core group consists of elected members, the organization itself has no rules or conditions for membership: all the district tribal women's organization's are its members, and through them it reaches the grassroots; it also supports local women's organizations in their efforts to stop violence.[10]

Like many other women's organizations in the country, the NMA too, started out as a group of mothers dealing with social problems, in particular alcohol abuse, drug addiction and AIDS. Through these, the mothers were able to mobilize women on a large scale and achieve considerable mass awareness in rural and urban areas. The NMA has set up a drug rehabilitation centre and an AIDS care hospice, among other charities. As an organization of mothers, the NMA has consistently underlined its mothering and healing character; its language of mobilizaiton revolves around motherhood, to the extent that it eschews formal political representation. Neidonuo Angama, immediate past president of NMA says, "We have our role to play as mothers, they (the men) have theirs."[11] When the NMA spoke out against "the simply intolerable way" that society was being run both by the Underground (UG) militants and the overground government, it said, "Mothers have the right to speak out and tell them (the leaders) what we want to say, whether they listen or not."[12] When interracial warfare between factions in Nagaland escalated alarmingly, the women's groups worked tirelessly to keep the channels of communication open between them. "All of them are our children, we care for them equally, though we do not support their differences," says a village woman elder in Jotsoma, Kohima district;[13] and when the NMA rushed to stem fratricidal violence in Phek district, Neidonuo Angama pleaded, "Before you kill your brother, listen to your mother."[14]

As with all other protracted armed conflict in South Asia, the long years of violence in Nagaland have thoroughly militarized and brutalized Naga society. State violence has been particularly relentless, with whole villages being razed to the ground; torture and encounter killings commonplace; rape and sexual assault routine; and any number of civilian killings and desecration of places of worship.[15]

The whole of Nagaland is under the Armed Forces (Special Powers) Act of 1958, the only state in the Indian Union to have been continuously subjected to it since 1995. Elsewhere in this study we have elaborated the widespread sexual violence against women by the armed forces in Nagaland; here we wish to focus on the protest against, and subsequent intervention by, the NMA on *all* violence in the state, in clear recognition of the fact that violence against women will not stop unless all other forms of violence also cease. And so, in August 1994, ten years after it was formed and departing from its earlier work of mobilizing on drugs, alcohol and AIDS, the NMA launched its "Shed No More Blood" campaign at its Fifth General Body Meeting in Zunheboto. The immediate cause for this plea was the growing number of unclaimed dead bodies lying in the bazaars and streets of towns and cities across the state.

The NMA came forward to honour the Naga tradition of giving every unclaimed body a dignified funeral, draped in the shawl of the tribe to which the deceased belonged. August 4, 1994 was designated Mourning Day by the NMA, and more than 3,000 mothers from various tribes attended this memorial meeting.[16] "Can we mothers remain silent, merely waiting to see who is the next victim?" they asked. Unmindful of their own safety, the mothers have prevented local boys from being taken into custody where they would certainly have been tortured or killed. On occasion they have negotiated with local commanding officers for their release, going so far as to stand surety for them. They have campaigned for the removal of army posts in towns and army camps in villages targeted by the Underground for spreading generalised fear and insecurity, especially among young girls.[17]

It would be fair to say that it was women's groups—all groups, including local organizations, the Naga Women's Union of Manipur (NWUM) and the NMA—who first protested large-scale human rights violations in the whole Naga territory, by both militants and the armed forces, especially cases of sexual assault and abuse. In Ukhrul district in 1974, for instance, when the army and paramilitary forces were accused of sexual violence against women, local village women got in touch with the district tribal women's organization and organized a mass mobilization for justice. Again, in a case of rape by two NSCN (National Socialist Council of Nagalim) cadres near the Jotsoma bypass in Kohima, the NMA coordinated a meeting between the victim's tribe and NSCN (I-M) leaders, following which action was taken against the offenders.

Violence against women apart, the NMA and other women's organizations have continued to highlight the escalation of all kinds of violence in the state; to negotiate—between the UG and the armed forces; between warring factions of the militants; between tribes; between the Kuki and Meiteis in Manipur; between women's groups—and to keep up a sustained dialogue on peace. In a public demonstration of this work the NMA organized a Peace Rally in Kohima in November 1995 on "Human Integrity and the Consequences of Killing". Ten members from each tribe participated, and representations were made to the Governor, the Chief Minister and the Commandant of Assam Rifles for the withdrawal of the Disturbed Areas Act. In particular, they expressed their disappointment at the lack of action on accusations of rape against the security forces.[18]

II

The tradition of Pukrelia among the Tangkhul tribe of Nagaland entailed the marriage of a woman from one tribe to a man from another, and goes back to the tribes' head-hunting days. The marriage signified a truce of sorts between them; the woman would intervene by stepping between the two tribes, stretching out her arms and declaring, "Stop, stop fighting. You on my brother's side, and you on my husband's side, stop fighting and let peace prevail for my sake." Rita Manchanda recounts how, in another version of Pukrelia "if two villages are at war and the death toll is rising, a wise woman has the prerogative to step forward and shake or whip open her *mekhala* (sarong), and by this shaming intervention stop the violence."[19]

The Naga Mothers' Association may not be the only association of mothers to have intervened or protested against violence by invoking the power and moral authority of the mother, but it was probably the first to do so in South Asia, and certainly the first in India. Curiously enough, they are still the only *mothers'* front to explicitly protest sexual violence against women. Admittedly, there is no shortage of women in the women's movement who are mothers and who also protest violence against women, but motherhood itself is neither the organizing principle underlying their campaigns, nor their primary identity. The Association of the Parents of Disappeared Persons in Kashmir, for instance, set up by Parveena Ahangar whose son has been missing since 1993, came into being many years after the NMA; even though its membership is largely female, it has a single point agenda: locating all missing persons, often in the hundreds or thousands, so that their families can either get them back or put a dignified closure to their lives. Much like the Mothers' Front in Jaffna (Sri Lanka).

The trajectory of the NMA's activism, however, is interesting and unusual for two important reasons: one, it rapidly gained social acceptance and commanded respect in a society where, traditionally, women have been excluded from public activity; and two, its role evolved from that of social worker (attacking alcoholism, drug abuse and AIDS) to becoming *social conscience*, i.e, demanding accountability *on behalf of society*, as mothers of the Naga community, from the state, from the armed forces and from the millitants. In short, they moved from *protest to active intervention,* very much in the public sphere, claiming that it was their *right* and their *duty* to stop the violence, to see that no more blood was shed.

Because they speak as mothers, claims Neidonuo Angami, they are trusted by everyone. Moreover, as Rita Manchanda has elaborated, their political language is an extension of their everyday life—they talk "kitchen politics", providing "a natural, non-threatening environment for facilitating dialogue in their kitchens, the heart of the Naga home".[20]

We do not have the space here to detail the process by which the NMA and NWUM have participated in and mediated the peace negotiations in Nagaland after the Accord of 1997, but one indication of their success is recognition by the Naga leadership of their contribution; at its Consultative Table, for instance, the NSCM (I-M) leaders have provided Naga women a seat because "we need them".[21]

The NMA's brand of activism, both protest and interventionary, against violence returns us once again to the question: is there such thing as women's practice of peace activism? If so, is this alternative protest and practice effective in the long run? Can it, for example, work across borders, regional, national or tribal?

As with economic activity, in peace work too, women belong in the informal sector, the informal spaces of politics, which by its very nature affects our practice. The ritualised cursing of the Mothers' Front or the sustained protest by the Mothers of the Plaza de Mayo, indeed the public mobilization of motherhood in the cause of peace and as a direct challenge to the state, are quintessentially "womanist" forms of peace activism. Bearing witness, as happens in the World Courts on Violence Against Women and in various tribunals on violence or other crimes, is not womanist in the same way, but it has radicalised the hitherto marginal and powerless and forced public and institutional notice outside the traditional arenas of such activity—the court, the police station, the executive or the bureaucracy.

Dialogue and networking have been among the most effective strategies used by the global women's movement in working for social change as well as in raising awareness. Dialogue that bridges difference and is predicated on respecting that difference is at the other end of the spectrum from what Ranabir Samaddar calls "maximalist friendship". Such a friendship, he says, "like cold war friendship depends on maximum enmity, and then maximum hostility".[22] Far from being conducive to peace, it kills understanding; it is this understanding that the NMA has been trying to forge. Trying, because as they themselves are the first to admit, they have not always been successful; there are serious reservations among the women on the NMA's role in specific cases of violence, and of course there are basic ideological differences between the NMA's motherhood politics and the NWUM's secular and progressive gender politics. Nevertheless, its contribution has been significant both in terms of strategy and as alternative practice.

Conclusion

The choice of three qualitatively different campaigns to illustrate alternative forms of protest and action, allows us to distinguish between them with regard to intent, scope and strategy.

The Railway Campaign as its name suggests, was triggered off by a specific incident, had a specific target, and could therefore make specific demands. The focus of the campaign was on unsafe travel for women on trains, the incidence of sexual assault and abuse, and the inability of the railways, the police and ultimately, the government machinery itself, to ensure the security of women passengers. This being so, the target of their protest was the same authorities: the Railway Protection Force, the Government Reserve Police and the Railway Ministry; and their demands were straightforward—safe travel for women; enabling mechanisms for reporting crimes against them on the railways, trains as well as platforms; and swift action against assaulters.

Thus far, the Campaign did not depart significantly from earlier protests on violence against women, whether on the streets, in custody or in public spaces. The notable differences lay in its strategising, and the forums through which it sought to mobilize both awareness of the issue, and administrative action. As discussed earlier, this time women's group sought an alliance with labour unions (specifically the railway employees' unions) on sexual violence against women, something of a first both for the women's movement and the trade union movement. Second, they petitioned the National Human Rights Commission, rather than the National Commission for Women, for redressal and intervention on their behalf with the Railway Ministry. In addition to its natural allies, then—women's wings of political parties, for example, or church-based organizations like the YWCA, and even other NGOs—this time the women's movement obtained the active support and participation of trade unions and mainstream media, in a conscious reformulation of its strategy.

Unfortunately, but predictably, the very nature of the beast has meant that despite some success, we have not been able to sustain the agitation beyond a point, nor been in a position to monitor compliance with the NHRC directives; as always institutional accountability remains elusive.

"War & Peace" on the other hand, was conceptualized very differently, and cannot even be said to constitute a "campaign" in the conventional sense. It makes no demands, indicts no single institution or event, and does not address a specific entity. It does not invite or require the participation of other groups, women's or otherwise, yet its "target" if you like, is society at large. If awareness raising can be said to prefigure protest, then the scope of "War & Peace" is expansive—it seeks to influence the general public, rural and urban, in its home state, Andhra Pradesh, and the rest of the country as well. Its decision to fan out into every district of the state and perform to audiences and settings far removed from the usual, was as innovative as the innovations it introduced in its chosen dance form. By no means was this the first time that the performative tradition had been used by the women's movement to make an alternative representation or to raise awareness; very early in our campaigning, the movement used street theatre to great effect in highlighting dowry murders and domestic violence. Songs, skits, one-acters and dramatic monologues have all been used at one time or another, but modifying myth and radicalising a classical dance or music tradition has not been attempted very much—in fact, it is rather rare.

Yet what could be better as a means of reaching out than epic literature, familiar to everyone across the country, told and retold thousands of times so that its every local variation and all its associations, religious and cultural, are immediately understood. Indeed, one might almost say that infusing myths with subversive content may well have a more far-reaching impact when presented outside the urban areas precisely because, often, the original is much better known there. In "War & Peace" the particularity of the myth or character is overcome by universal acceptance and boldness of execution. Its message is clear: once conscientised, women will no longer be silent, they will speak the violence that has been done to them, whether in war or in peace.

The singular and startling contribution of the NMA lies in its assertion that the *whole of society* is a victim of violence in Nagaland; that as mothers, their concern is with everyone, they cannot be partisan in their condemnation. Moreover, as Paula Banerjee has pointed out, the NMA has democratized the peace process by "keeping the two protagonists in the negotiations, the Indian government and the NSCN (IM) accountable to the Naga people's desire for peace". Because they have defined peace differently by associating it with justice and development, she believes they have been more successful in their efforts at forming peace groups, and in surviving over a long period.[23] Though the Mothers cannot be called feminist by any means, their stand on violence has been unequivocal. Consequently, of the three campaigns discussed here, theirs has been the longest running; we would argue that because of this and because it embraces society as a whole, their transition from protest to intervention has been far more clearly articulated and realised. It has also allowed them to enter the political arena through the peace process, another advance on their earlier reluctance to be political.

Like myth, the powerful charge of motherhood has

been used by the NMA to mobilize women—rural, urban, tribal, Christian—across the state in their mission to end violence. "We appeal to them as mothers, that we should all work for peace because if a child dies, it touches us, it grieves us. Because for a mother anybody's child is our child."[24] But these mothers, unlike many others in the region, have reached the negotiating table, primarily because they did not hesitate to intervene on behalf of everyone—women, militants, the government.

Through their action and their mobilizing the NMA has not only validated a completely alternative and domestic "kitchen politics", they have signalled an alternative way of doing politics *and* peace, one that is nonviolent, democratic and consensual.

Notes & references

[1] "Back on Track! The Railway Campaign" (New Delhi: Jagori and sundry women's organizations, 2002).
[2] "The Railway Campaign: Fighting Sexual Violence on Trains," *Manushi*, Issue 130.
[3] All details regarding the Railway Campaign are taken from the two accounts and documents cited. See also "Looking Back: The Railway Campaign," (New Delhi: Jagori, 2002).
[4] Order dated March 9, 1999 to the Chief Security Commissioners, RPF, All Zonal Railways.
[5] Excerpted from the Newsletter published by the NHRC, March 2002.
[6] "The Railway Campaign," op. cit.
[7] Arijit Barman, "On the Tracks", *Outlook*, April 2, 2001. Other reports appeared in the *Times of India*, April 2002, and online sites like Indiatogether.
[8] Naila Kabeer, "From Feminist Insights to an Analytical Framework", in Naila Kabeer and Ramya Subramanian, *Institutions, Relations and Outcomes: A Framework and Case Studies for Gender-aware Planning* (New Delhi: Kali for Women, 1999).
[9] *The Sunday Mumbai Newsline*, May 1, 2005.
[10] For a synoptic history of the NMA see Paula Banerjee, "Between Two Armed Patriarchies: Women in Assam and Nagaland", in Rita Manchanda (ed.), *Women, War and Peace in South Asia: Beyond Victimhood to Agency* (New Delhi: Sage, 2001).
[11] Rita Manchanda, *We do More Because We Can: Naga Women in the Peace Process* (Kathmandu: South Asia Forum for Human Rights, 2004), p. 28.
[12] Ibid., p. 27.
[13] Ibid., p. 43.
[14] Ibid., p. 43.
[15] See Paula Banerjee and Rita Manchanda, op. cit., and Anuradha M. Chenoy, "Implications of Insurgencies on Women: India," unpublished report prepared for the Regional Centre of Social Studies, Colombo.
[16] Rita Manchanda, "We do More..." op. cit., p. 45.
[17] Ibid., p. 38.

[18] Ibid., p. 45.
[19] Ibid., p. 23.
[20] For a detailed account of the NMA's role in the peace process in Nagaland, see Paula Banerjee and Rita Manchanda, op. cit.
[21] Rita Manchanda, " We do More...", op. cit., p. 78.
[22] Ranabir Samaddar, "Friends, Foes and Understanding", unpublished paper.
[23] Paula Banerjee, op. cit., pp. 162–173.
[24] Rita Manchanda, "We do More..." op. cit., p. 62.

4 Feminist Interventions

Kalpana Kannabiran

THIS chapter looks at the ways in which violence against women has been acted against by groups and institutions, autonomous as well as state—as part of a larger feminist initiative. There are four parts to this exercise. The first part consists of a broad overview of interventions in different states in India on issues drawn primarily from the reflections and work of women who are part of feminist collectives in Assam, Tripura, West Bengal, Orissa, Kerala, Andhra Pradesh, Karnataka and Tamil Nadu; the second part looks at public hearings as a method of bearing collective witness to violence and violation that women have experienced; the third part examines in depth the solidarity campaign for Bhanwari Devi, gang-raped for attempting to stop child-marriages in Rajasthan; the fourth deals with mass mobilization, particularly the anti-arrack struggle in Andhra Pradesh that focussed on the issue of domestic violence. The concluding section summarises the nationwide mobilization and campaigns that galvanized support for anti-violence campaigns by Dalit women, using the frameworks of international human rights law—with specific reference to the processes around the Convention on the Elimination of Racial Discrimination (CERD) and the National Federation of Dalit Women. The purpose of this chapter is to demonstrate the diversity of interventions that feminists have used in anti-violence work.

I

This section focuses on the everyday politics of feminism in India, and its persistent attempt at advancing substantive feminist goals. This politics delineates methodological tools and frameworks to comprehend, explain and change iniquitous, endemically violent realities. Feminist methods therefore advance feminist goals by addressing historiography, the politics of organizing at different levels, and writing anti-discrimination and anti-violence commitments into legal systems that have either forgotten them or wiped them out.

Media sensitivity

Print media's response to violence against women began gaining visibility in local and national mainstream media in the 1980s. The dominant problems identified at the time were dowry deaths and bigamy in Hindu families; housewives and professional women alike rallied around these and other issues. Resistance took various forms (demonstrations, meetings, street theatre and critical writing), and women's organizations from the Left were also part of this mobilizing. Their visibility today is a continuation of the process that began then, although in the intervening period there has been a change in how media represents that violence. The number of stories and news space allotted to the issue have gone up significantly, as has the number of women reporters, journalists, news producers and film-makers. Yet this does not necessarily indicate greater awareness within the media about violence as an issue related to social justice or equality; despite any number of initiatives directed at media sensitisation, it continues to be seen as primarily a "women's issue".

The stand of the vernacular press remains ambivalent, varying only in degree depending on the target readership. In subtle and direct ways the vernacular press in Bengal, for example, represented community policing to a great extent, foregrounding the issue of morality in most reported cases other than sexual violence. Domestic battering could thus be perfectly "justified" on grounds of suspected transgression. While the number of sexual violence cases being reported has increased, follow-up is dismal; crimes continue unabated and are, in fact, on the rise, compounded by structural factors.[1]

As often as not, media coverage of violence has sensationalised the issue and catered to the commercial interests of the media agency. However, even mere coverage has served an important purpose, leading to a debate within women's groups and to their consolidation along informal as well as institutional lines.

The question of how violated women are represented by the media, is equally significant. Where women survivors are concerned, once the decision in favour of disclosure is made, communication is simple. It is generally a statement of what happened to them, spoken in the language they know. The fact that language itself is coded against direct disclosure, that words collapse honour and sexual experience in ways that make it impossible to separate one from the other, are problems that both limit women's access to media, as well as their access to justice, even today. Rape, for instance, is almost never named directly except in the law; it is always expressed through euphemisms that either downplay the violence or sensationalise it, depending on the position of the victim-survivor. In that sense nothing has changed since Mathura. Even so, women speak. The problem is that they do not speak in capsules, they do not tell us everything in one sitting. They do not begin with the most painful, most injurious experiences, and neither their pain nor their experience can be "captured" on camera in a single frame. In the course of the telling they peel off layer after layer, and it is all of this that is their story.

Most stories of violence that have been reported in Asmita over the last fifteen years have been spread over months, sometimes even a year or more, sometimes only "incidentally", when the stated purpose of seeking help is to prevent eviction or dispossession. In some cases women have made their peace with extreme abuse, reckoning that the environment outside might be more hostile to them, perhaps even more violent than the home. It may be illustrative to look at exactly how complicated the issue can be through the experience of a few specific cases of violence against women.[2]

After twenty years of daily sexual abuse and marital rape, Priyamvada decided not to go ahead with divorce proceedings, and stated in writing that "nothing had happened". While handing over the letter, she observed with an expressionless face that one must not lose faith in the possibility of even the worst criminal turning good.

At what cost do women find peace, and what kind of peace do they find? Sometimes, women have died without reconciliation, insisting that their bodies not be handed over to the family that deserted them while they were alive. When Varalakshmi realised that she would die alone and uncared for in a small hospital at the edge of town, she was categorical in her assertion that her body not be given to her husband and children. When they heard this, the latter went to court and procured an order in their favour, because the judge felt the woman's soul "must rest in peace", that she should not lie unclaimed, to be disposed off by the municipality. But she was unclaimed in life, having battled destitution and desertion after leading a relatively comfortable life; and having coped with children and husband pressing charges of insanity when her demand for livelihood support, based on real estimates of a reasonable, healthy life, was persistent.

There are others like Gloria who, having been sexually assaulted and abused by their husbands for many years, escape, leaving behind infant children. Years later, they decide to revisit the past and press for divorce and custody of their children, on grounds of cruelty. Where is the space in our field of vision to account for the fact that it might actually take a woman eight long years to be able to return to the site of violence and decide to act on that experience?

The accretion of violence, with the only remedy that most women have against it being *more* violence, negation and denial, how will these stories ever be told in the media? How long will the media wait to hear a story? What will be retained and what edited out as inconsequential or irrelevant? Mainstream media are impatient. This impatience has to do with the public domain itself, which is structured in ways that actively excludes certain classes of people, and where dominant hegemonies are all-pervasive. In such a context, all those classes and marginalized groups that are not participant/perpetrators are kept invisible; exceptions are made only when visibility is rendered in terms of the dominant discourse—the media then represents the experience in the space/time/method that is predetermined. In attempting alternate representations, therefore, what one is actually doing is whittling away the edifice of hegemonic patriarchy, something that, in its very doing, is unlikely to find favour.

Feminist interventions in case-work have therefore focussed on creating and nurturing a sensitivity in the media at different levels towards the experiences of women, as well as creating alternative news services that solicit and carry stories that are sympathetic to the complexities of these experiences.

Sensitising the criminal justice machinery

The criminal justice system has been critical to feminist interventions from the late 1970s. Beginning with the movement against custodial rape and violence, feminist campaigning placed the question of sexual assault within the framework of state violence for the first time, drawing attention to its patriarchal underpinnings, and examining the processes through which violence and masculinity lock women into abusive situations that spill over the public-private divide in startlingly similar ways. At the time when early feminist interventions on custodial rape were most vocal, whether on Mathura or Rameeza Bi, resistance against other practices of impunity, the torture and extra-judicial killings of men in political struggles and resistance movements was also at its peak, immediately after the Emergency of 1975. In an important sense, therefore, feminist interventions shared common ground with human rights movements on the specific issue of civil and political rights, with custodial rape becoming the defining characteristic of the torture of women in custody.

Not surprisingly, then, one sees a strong coalition in the early years between human rights groups and emergent women's groups on the issue of state violence. In raising it, the focus may have been primarily on sexual assault, but the articulation of difference and diversity was implicit in the very process of searching for remedy and redress through the courts and commissions of enquiry. This analysis would become much more thoroughgoing in the following years. The focus on the victim's character, immorality, and the problem of consent that were the centrepoints of debate around Rameeza and Mathura, highlighted their experiences in the context of their specific identities as Muslim and adivasi women. In Rameeza's case, particularly, the judge, Justice Muktadar, an affluent Muslim who constituted the one-man commission of enquiry, went on record to say that the case had opened his eyes to the plight of poor Muslim women in the country. The fact that the criminal justice system does not discern the specificity of women's interaction with it, merely treats them in certain ways because they have come into contact with it, raises serious questions about limitations in the meaning of justice for women within patriarchal (albeit democratic) systems.

It soon became evident that the problem of violence did not stop with women who were victims of sexual assault and domestic violence; it also affected women who were apprehended and placed under custody. The focus now shifted from custodial violence to the question of reforms in women's jails, and to working among women prisoners on a more regular basis. Testimonies of women in custody clearly establish their absolute powerlessness as they face trial. Although in need of enormous support from families and legal counsel in order to navigate dense legal procedures, in reality they receive almost no advice on how to present their case and respond to the evidence produced. Providing sureties for women undertrials or those convicted for petty offences has been a major feminist intervention. A close examination of the case records of women prisoners reveals extreme vulnerability, deprivation and desperation that pushes them to kill family members, including children; within the criminal justice system itself, however, there is a complete capitulation to stereotypes that swing between protectionist and misogynist constructions of women's position and agency.

Elaborating this point in hindsight, it is useful to revisit the early period of feminist interventions by posing a set of questions: Are women victims or survivors of domestic violence? If they are survivors of custodial violence, how did they happen to come into custody? Were they just picked up for no ostensible reason? Did they find themselves in custody for violating norms in the private space of the family? Did they end up in custody for allegedly committing hard crimes like murder? Are these women victim-survivors of collective/public violence? Does why they find themselves in custodial spaces matter? Is there any rational connection between the reason and the consequence? Is the disjuncture between reason and consequence—or even the absence of disjuncture between state custody and conjugal/familial custody—symbolic of the predicament of women, across differences?

Keeping the struggle going

Conversations with feminists in different parts of the country and a review of their work on violence foregrounds its familiar, yet uneasy, repetitiveness. Providing resources, shelter or legal services; researching their lack; sensitising judicial officers, the police and communities to the criticality of work around and against violence; campaigning for justice in a particular case, often unsuccessfully; campaigning for reform in legislation and finding that, often, the reformed law is made to stand on its head; are the constants of our resistance. While reform represents a major feminist intervention, what we have learnt from it is to understand and interpret the silence, complicity and active undermining of justice claims through a coalition of dominant interests. There has been little or no change in the attitude of the state and its agencies, viz., the police and the judiciary, towards violence against women. At best violated women are looked upon as victims, in rare cases as survivors; by and large, society (aided by the media) still holds a woman responsible for her situation. Clearly, this is something that is deeply problematic for feminists; yet, it is necessary to chip away at structures of dominance and rupture them, albeit in small ways. Organizing meetings, training programmes and interactive sessions with the bureaucracy, especially the police and the judiciary, are part of this effort.

The critique, even within the movement, that these interventions are palliative and cannot in any fundamental way bring about a shift in women's lived experiences of structural violence and inequality, is not unjustified. The fact that these programmes interrogate assumptions of the just state, as well as of equal citizenship, by underscoring the responsibility of individual incumbents in governance to deliver the constitutional mandate, must remain in focus. Forcing the judiciary to confront its assumption that the letter and spirit of the law is self-evident; forcing it into a position where it is not merely delivering a verdict but learning from victim support groups instead, is a process fraught with resistance because it inverts the cultural paradigms that uphold the position of the infallible judge, and the performance of obeisance and obedience that go with them. The rest, of course, must be left to an independent, self-generating process of reflexivity that several feminist groups believe has set in, consequent to these efforts.

Apart from the consciousness of incumbents, there is the larger issue of the environment within which violence against women is embedded. Forty years ago, the Santhanam Committee, in its report of the Committee on the Prevention of Corruption, observed that "corruption has increased to such an extent that people have started losing faith in the integrity of the public administration. . . The very fact that such impressions are there causes damage to the social fabric."[3] Discussions on the jurisprudence of corruption focus on jurisprudence publique and the folklore of bribal cultures that speak to dramas in the corridors of power. The persistent failure of women to access justice underscores the need to further develop this jurisprudence of corruption to include women's experiences of it, especially the criminal justice system. The case of Bhanwari Devi, for instance, demonstrates the lack of congruence between the definition of magnitude in terms of economic cost and political stakes in a predominantly masculine world of hard politics, and the definition in terms of magnitude of impact on the life situations of survivors. Their encounter with corruption is in the betrayal of justice by those who are entrusted to it—*coitus politicus* is the convergence of masculine power and justice, the guarantee of impunity to the perpetrators of violence against women.[4] It is important to raise the issue of corruption at the beginning of this section, because the fact of a corrupt administration forms the background, and the battleground, that women survivors and their supporters must navigate and contend with.

Global developments, marketisation and privatisation have pushed women into new forms of trafficking, like sex tourism, in addition to existing traditional forms of prostitution. The liberalisation of the Indian economy has vastly diminished traditional livelihoods for the poor. The conversion of large tracts of agricultural land for commercial aqua production, the diminishing viability of traditional livelihood skills, the lack of education or skills for alternative means of income, have resulted in large numbers of women having no other option but to enter the sex trade. The issue of trafficking has become increasingly visible in anti-violence interventions. Despite this, however, levels of public knowledge and awareness on it remain rudimentary, with most people conflating trafficking with prostitution. Ironically, while there is an increase in the number of agencies and networks engaged in this critical intervention, and while the academic and theoretical debate on the issue has gained considerable ground,[5] the problem itself continues to grow at an alarming pace. One troubling aspect of work against trafficking is that public debates on the issue have begun to erode resources allocated for direct intervention, a factor that may account for our failure to tackle the problem effectively.

Because marriage is an important conduit for trafficking, feminist and other interventions have had to work with families who no longer have contact with married daughters, in an attempt to trace them. This meets with understandable resistance as it militates against the very ideology of marriage. It is not uncommon to find survivors being re-trafficked, or consenting to being "married" or sold again. This happens when the community is reluctant to accept and accommodate the survivor, or if she is unable to secure a livelihood or dignified existence amongst her own. To some extent her first experience creates a self-exploitative tendency in her; anything appears to be more acceptable and promising than the difficult conditions she is already in.[6]

The specific patterns of violence against women vary, depending on the socio-cultural and economic conditions of the region. In Orissa, for example, large tracts of tribal areas, normally governed by customary practices, are now exposed to law enforcing agencies like the police, Central Reserve Police Force (CRPF) and the army. The greater the power these bodies wield, the greater the violence they are able to inflict if tribal communities dare to protest their oppressive presence. Such violations have grown in recent years because forests, forest produce and the abundant manpower available in these areas make for lucrative business propositions. Tribals are dispossessed, exploitation becomes the norm, and as is bound to happen, women bear the brunt of the violence. The rape of tribal women in the reserve forest area of Banpur led to the women themselves conducting organized protests, making the issue public and demanding justice.[7]

Over a period of three decades, feminist groups that provide support to victim-survivors of domestic violence have found that criminal remedies alone are inadequate in dealing with the enormity of violence, and patriarchal oppression and exclusion. Criminal remedies on maintenance, for instance, did not recognize women's contribution to the building and sustenance of the shared matrimonial home. Whereas the quantification of women's household labour impacted on policy and resulted in significant shifts in census enumeration, it had no impact whatsoever on the *judicial* perception of women's entitlements at work or at home. We contend that the whittling down and undermining of women's claims happens through the patriarchal strategy of disaggregation, so that although everything is intimately connected, nothing ever adds up. If some feminist interventions in favour of the Domestic Violence Act have attempted to effect this convergence, others have found that they are themselves victims of disaggregation; how, for instance, would one quantify economic abuse as the refusal of a husband to contribute to family maintenance?[8]

There has been some change in general attitudes on the issue of the sexual abuse of girls and children. Schools and other institutions have moved from an initial stance of resistance to gradual acceptance, to a proactive engagement with the issue. This is more evident in missionary schools and colleges. However, we have a long way to go as far as sensitising members of the administrative machinery is concerned. The example of the existing law on rape making no distinction between adult and minor rape, is a case in point.[9]

The experiences of women in areas of armed conflict presents an alarming scenario in which they are at the receiving end of domestic and economic violence, armed ethnic conflict, cross-border displacement, state-engineered conflicts, and poverty-and-unemployment-induced trafficking. If we were to take the specific example of the north-eastern region of India, we would note that the violence is multi-layered and nuanced. There is "armed conflict" and resultant state repression; there are inter-tribal, inter-group, linguistic, cultural and other conflicts; there are intra-group conflicts caused by the clash of modern ideas with traditional systems within groups; and then there is the general violence in society caused by the growing inequities of uneven development and unequal opportunities. At the intersection of all this is the woman who must maintain a livelihood, and sustain the family, as well.

As in other armed conflict zones, here too the body of the woman is used to establish control and take revenge. The draconian Armed Forces (Special Powers) Act allows for violent combing operations, search and seizure, and open firing; intermittently over the last three decades, almost every state in the north-east has been under the AFSPA and military occupation for long periods of time.[10] Violence against women across the board has been affected by the larger conflict here which has blocked development, hampered normal living, led to anti-people laws and policies, and to high levels of discontent and resentment among the youth. Health personnel refuse to go to conflict-torn regions; women in need of medical care refuse to come out for fear of the security forces. Absence of livelihood options exposes them to violence and exploitation at the hands of anyone with the slightest control over their lives. Living under constant fear and dread is a kind of violence that has a lasting impact on the minds and bodies of women and young girls; all interventions in this area, whether feminist, human rights or humanitarian, have been at the initiative of NGOs or civil society groups. Among the first-named, the women's organization, North-East Network, has been working in a sustained way for over ten years now, with remarkable dedication. Feminist interventions in conflict zones have been in the nature of networking, confidence-building, providing services and sometimes even shelter, where required.

Finally, a significant part of feminist intervention has been pedagogic, incorporating the discussion of violence against women within curricula, particularly in the social sciences and humanities; the mid-1990s saw several efforts at addressing this issue in all its complexity within the academy.

II

We are half the sky

In 2004, an election year for Andhra Pradesh, a group of eight women's, human rights, and development organizations came together to plan how to reclaim International Women's Day. This had lapsed into a cliché-ridden mode, with campaigns being run by governments and the corporate sector alike, completely depoliticising the meaning of freedom for women. As a resistance to the increasingly hostile environments in which women must constantly live and negotiate, women's groups in AP felt the need to organize in larger numbers, specifically on the issue of violence against women, coming together on a common platform to raise women's concerns more effectively. The strategy was to collect around 5,000 women in the heart of the capital to demonstrate their powerful presence and their political priorities to those who chose to watch. The events of March 7 and 8, 2004, were thus planned expressly to reclaim the articulation of women's rights and their right to expression, and consisted of workshops on trafficking, domestic violence and women's representation in local bodies, as well as a public hearing on violence against women. Eighty-six organizations from across the state participated in this two-day meet, which was an assertion of women's right to define their struggles, and a demand for their voices be heard.

By midday on Sunday, March 7, the Nizam College grounds, in the heart of the city, were brimming with women who had left their homes and families to speak up for their rights. They entered the grounds, babes in arms and bags clutched firmly. Food stalls and water counters were brisk and busy as women refreshed themselves after their journey and headed for the plenary session. By 1.00 p.m. the plenary hall was packed with 5,000 women. On the agenda was a public hearing on violence against women, with survivors of extreme assault bearing testimony to their violence, compelling the 5,000 strong gathering to acknowledge their violation. The cases spanned a wide range of issues; four of the women witnessed and suffered extreme violence in their childhood—three of them still children, with one, Sulochana, having grown to adulthood with memories of brutal assault by upper caste Kamma landlords, in which her husband was killed when she was just thirteen years old.

Karamchedu and Chunduru are violent reminders of the violence of caste. In Karamchedu, this is what happened: on July 16, 1985, at about 3.30 p.m., a Kamma boy was washing his buffalo on the steps of the water tank of the Dalits, and letting the soiled water out into the tank. A disabled Dalit youth objected to this. The Kamma boy reacted violently and beat him with a cattle-whip. A young Dalit woman who had come to fetch water protested the beating, and was also whipped and kicked.[11] On July 17, hundreds of Kammas from the same and neighbouring villages, armed with axes, spears and clubs, attacked the Dalits; six Dalits were murdered; three women raped and many more wounded, some of them critically; their huts burnt, and whatever little was with them, looted.

Sulochana was thirteen years old and had recently been married when the Karamchedu massacre took place. The day the trouble started, she went to wash clothes in the pond as usual, and was caught in the violence on her return home. She received grievous injuries on the head and spent two months in hospital, recovering. She was witness to the massacre and saw several people being attacked and killed. Later she learnt that her husband was one among them. All the accused in the Karamchedu incident were acquitted; in Sulochana's words, the high court judge found the details of the incident "unbelievable". Sulochana's courage and her willingness to share memories of unspeakable terror and irreparable loss, and her faith in the possibility of a better world, renewed the faith of those gathered in the value of sharing and speaking out as feminist strategies. That the caste massacres at Karamchedu in 1985 and Chunduru in 1991 have had the guarantee of impunity raise serious questions about the possibility of justice in the present political order. Although Karamchedu happened nineteen years earlier it came alive on March 7, 2004, both because of

Sulochana's testimony, and because twelve years after the Chunduru massacre, survivors are still fighting for the right to a fair trail while the accused go scot free. The scale on which this happens signifies not just atrocity, but a crime against humanity.

Rape and sexual assault are forms of violence that survivors, judges and lawyers hesitate to name, because they entail the horror of social ostracism for the victim-survivor. It has needed exceptional courage for women to be able to even register cases of rape. Thirteen-year-old Madhavi's strength in reporting her rape and assisting investigating agencies in apprehending the accused was remarkable and inspiring; even more energising was her ability to appear before 5,000 women, all adults, and speak without fear, teaching every one of us to be fearless in our pursuit of justice.

Similarly Karuna, aged 15, has been steady in her resolve to press charges against an abusive father, even replacing her family with a new community of support at Ankuram. When it is so difficult to grapple with the impact of disclosure on family "honour," Karuna demonstrated the meaning of kinship, community and care, and reiterated powerfully that abuse is abuse, whether by father or stranger, and must be treated as such. This interpretation stands in stark contrast to the equivocation by law-enforcing agencies. Child sexual abuse within the family—another form of custodial violence—has been one of the most complex issues to tackle for feminists. If comprehension is the first step in dealing with abuse, coping is the next, since it is rarely possible for victims to remove themselves immediately from an abusive situation. The most painful part of abuse then, is the period when the victim knows s/he is in constant danger of being abused again, and continues to experience it, or live in perpetual fear, because there is no immediate remedy. Disclosure is also most difficult in these cases, because it is usually made to other members of the family, all of whom inevitably counsel tolerance and forgiveness.

Dubashi Manjula was the first Dalit woman sarpanch of her village in Medak, a district crippled by caste and untouchability. She has been assaulted several times, paraded on the streets of her village, abused and denied her powers as sarpanch—for having the courage to first contest and win an election, and then insist on governing the village. In a country where corruption scandals run into crores of rupees every year, Dalit women are denied cheque-signing powers on the ground that they cannot keep correct accounts. The real story, however, is that money is withdrawn by upper caste landlords through the routine use of forged signatures. What are the safeguards we must insist upon for women, especially Dalit women, in governance? What are the measures we must take to ensure that women complete their terms in office with all their powers and responsibilities intact?

The different layers in which violence is embedded; the indispensability of the painful exercise of peeling off each layer through which the impact of violence penetrates in order to "see" and cope with the impact; through which memory must trawl in order to capture the full meaning of the experience, make survival and recovery a daunting task. The first way of dealing with abuse, it is said, is to "speak out": disclosure as a one-shot, blowing-the-lid-off-abuse tactic in the hope that the law will take charge the moment we speak out. But disclosure is as multi-layered and multi-textured as the violence itself, and the "law" (assuming, of course, that we mean a *secular* law) hovers above, barely touching the surface, and even then reluctantly. We learn that the law also "copes" with family violence, caste violence, sexual abuse and assault and larger processes of discrimination through dissociation, providing little relief or opportunity for recuperation to survivors.

Five thousand women watched and heard spellbound as women recounted their experiences of horror and violence, while the jury spoke about the need to connect their experiences to what was happening outside—coming to grips with poverty, fundamentalism, caste and domestic violence, underscoring the need to understand the intersections between different kinds of violence in women's lives.

III

This section will discuss the rape of Bhanwari Devi, a development worker, as an example of a larger exercise of hegemonic power over not just women, but feminist politics. At the outset it must be stated that the reason why Bhanwari's case is important is because it embodies the risk-taking that feminist politics involves. Till this point, campaigns around rape spoke of the extreme vulnerability of women in families, communities and societies, and of the need for feminist groups to rally round and support victim-survivors in their quest for justice. With the Bhanwari case, the focus shifts from the victim-survivor to the feminist agent of social transformation, on whose person the marks of conservatism and patriarchal control are inscribed; sexual assault becomes a tool for containing and undermining feminist politics.

In the year 1984, the Women's Development Programme was set up in Rajasthan by the Government of India, with the primary objective of empowering rural women to play an active role in development. Bhanwari, from village Bhateri, was *recruited* as a *saathin*, or community worker, in the programme in 1985. As part of its work on development, the programme took up issues related to local government, land, water, the public distribution system, minimum wages, health, literacy—and child marriage. (It should be mentioned here that the state of Rajasthan accounts for the highest percentage of child marriages—almost 60 per cent—in the country.) Clearly, while these were "issues" to be worked on, they were also deeply connected to the lives of the *saathins* themselves. Child marriage, for instance, was discussed for the first time in Bhateri as part of the programme in 1986. Bhanwari and the other *saathins*, prior to joining the programme, had themselves got their daughters married before they attained puberty. Discussing the issue in the programme forced a deeper reflection on it by the *saathins*, and they agreed to postpone the *gauna* (post-pubertal ritual signalling co-habitation) of their daughters. Bhanwari began to educate her own daughter, who had also been married as a child but had still not gone through the *gauna*. By 1989 Bhanwari established her presence as an activist who had taken up a range of issues, from organizing the panchayat to rapes in her village, and had been identified as a full-time trainer by the WDP.

In 1992, seven years after Bhanwari joined the programme, the government decided to observe an anti-child marriage fortnight between April and May, when most such marriages take place. In an effort to make the campaign more effective, Bhanwari identified persons in the village with young girl children who, in her view, needed to be dissuaded from getting them married. Ram Karan Gujar, a ward panch with a one-year old daughter, was the first person Bhanwari approached, although village elders were clearly angry with her for raising the issue with them. Undeterred, the project director and senior police officials followed up on Bhanwari's visit, actively preventing the marriage. Tension mounted in Bhateri and the men of the village, not just of the Gujar caste but even Bhanwari's own father-in-law, held her directly responsible for the police action. Bhanwari and her husband were assaulted and abused, but she refrained from lodging a police complaint lest the situation worsen.

The abuse of Bhanwari was physical, verbal and economic—her trees were cut, fodder stolen, and the postmaster who employed her, assaulted. Meetings to resolve the tension were largely unsuccessful. Finally in June, two months after the incident, the pressure on Bhanwari eased and there was some semblance of normalcy in her life between June and September. Then, on September 22, Bhanwari's husband was assaulted and she herself gang-raped in the fields, while at work, by two upper caste men, Gyarsa Gujar and Badri Gujar. It was clear that all parties in the village had two positions on the issue of child marriage: while they campaigned for its abolition, they continued to perform marriages in their own homes. This was true even of Badri Gujar, one of the men who had raped Bhanwari.[12]

Bhanwari's attempt to reconcile rhetoric with

practice threw her society into crisis. However, it is important to examine the entire case in the light of feminist methods of organizing. It is true that Bhanwari was campaigning against child marriage—the contradiction is that she was doing this as part of her job, not as part of feminist political organizing. It is this contradiction that enables an understanding of the complete rupture between women's groups and the government (in its large monolithic form) after the assault on Bhanwari. In a very fundamental sense, it is deeply problematic to cast a campaign against child marriage as work-related, parti-cularly because it involves a persuasive, deliberative politics that spreads beyond workday or job descriptions. Where there is an acknowledgement of the criticality of this work by the government, the methodology of the programme must be defined by the persons engaged in it at the community level, rather than by resorting to the use of force—arbitrary both in its use and in its withdrawal.

It has been argued that feminist politics follows the method of practical reasoning which characterizes feminists' engagement on issues as well as with the law. Clearly, for Bhanwari, the problem of child marriage was not one of dichotomised conflict, but a predicament fraught with contradictions and multiple perspectives, something she could recognize because of her own belated awareness of the "problem". The solution therefore lay in persuasion, which would no doubt create anger and tension, but could be resolved with further persuasion. Dispersed as the problem was—not confined to a single caste, not a problem created by men alone but one that adult women participated in as well—

the solution, it would appear, lay in "imaginative integrations and reconciliations", which require attention to particular contexts. (The context is clearly understood as the context of politics in all its complexity.) "The *saathins* prefer to work through persuation [sic] and are against any police action because it makes people hostile and impedes the *saathins'* work."[13] People's unwillingness, their anger, their dishonesty even, would present solutions in the ultimate analysis, because new situations are generative and enable practical perceptions.[14]

To intervene in this situation with the brutal might of the state and attempt to handle it with police action, disintegrates and disables a carefully crafted political programme that might have a potential not immediately visible—after all, it was possible for Bhanwari to decide not to perform her daughter's *gauna* but educate her instead. It was also possible for her to actually take up a case of rape in her village. Even after the police action, she refrained from registering an FIR when she and her husband were harassed, in the hope that her restraint would retrieve the situation in her favour.[15] What she had not anticipated was that the moment the contentious politics of masculinity and power came into play, the use of coercive police action on communities [without reference to her] would evoke moral policing by the community through the use of brute force, in this instance sexual assault. Within this logic of *coitus politicus*, no redress is in fact possible for women on the ground, even when protections exist on paper. The masculinity of state policing is matched by the masculinity of community policing, both of which converge.

This was not the first time that women were victims in battles between state agencies and caste communities; rather, state action fused communities into a common purpose, in a situation that was otherwise bitterly divided along caste lines. As early as June 1992, three months before Bhanwari was assaulted, her father-in-law called a Kumhar jati panchayat which excommunicated her.[16] Clearly, while the state initiated action against them, elected representatives and MLAs condemned the action and demonstrated support for the Gujars. Although the spontaneous feminist response to Bhanwari's experience characterized the assault as a retaliation to her work against child marriage, a closer examination of the case reveals a more complex configuration of power and politics.

When Bhanwari was assaulted no one in the village was willing to support her. The police were reluctant to register her complaint, even asking if she knew the meaning of "rape". Doctors were not available in primary health centres, although Bhanwari knew that she could not change her clothes and had to go through the necessary steps in order to see her case through the court. Feminist practical reasoning, it would seem from Bhanwari's actions, urges a bonding between reason and emotion, even at the most difficult times. With support only from her husband (himself a victim of assault) and her co-workers in the campaign, scattered in different villages, Bhanwari was medically examined 47 hours after she was assaulted. What came into play was the immediate convergence of interests between community, police, judiciary, state-run medical services and the executive, a complicity which cannot be understated as "negligence".[17] It is necessary to unpack this convergence and complicity, both its perpetration and the guarantee of impunity. They marked Bhanwari's journey from Bhateri to Jaipur over four days, ending in her having to deposit the skirt she was wearing at the Bassi police station as evidence, and walking three kilometers to a *saathin's* village draped in her husband's chadar.

One month after Bhanwari was raped, when still no action had been initiated against the accused, *saathins* got together at a public meeting to speak out—not just in solidarity with Bhanwari, but about their own experiences of assault that, till then, had remained private. The point is not that violence against women is a common experience—violence is our context—but that remedy and redress, consequent on feminist activism, were possible for offences that were similar in form. What was it that set Bhanwari apart? What was the source of hostility in her environment? Is it possible that the anger of communities against the state was deflected onto Bhanwari; and the anger of the state at the effectiveness of feminist activism that surpassed its own practice of politics? This effectively disabled any convergence of interests and solidarities, returning us to our earlier question: can a campaign against child marriage be carried out as part of paid work in the larger context of a convergence of state and non-state patriarchies?

In terms of the resolution, the trajectory of practical reasoning opens up spaces for negotiation within particular contexts where women live and work. While antagonism can take the form of extreme violence against women activists, Bhanwari made the difficult choice to return to Bhateri and renegotiate her position by calling a jati panchayat in 1993. There was hostility, of course, (her father-in-law claimed she had pushed him into a well); there was suspicion (she had just received Rs. 10,000 as compensation from the Prime Minister's Relief Fund); and there was isolation (she had had no social contact with anybody in the village).[18] Yet, she called a panchayat, not for delivering justice because she had been sexually assaulted, but to restore her to her own context, with dignity. Since that context is specific, and she alone was a part of it, she made it clear that no member of her support group be present at that meeting. Reading this as capitulation to forces of dominance and violence would be rather simplistic, given Bhanwari's own history of doing feminist politics.

In February 1995 Bhanwari, along with twelve women from Prempura and Bhateri villages, decided to participate in the meeting of the newly elected Bhateri panchayat consisting of five villages. Among those elected were four women—one Dalit, one adivasi and two Brahmin. To her surprise, the newly elected sarpanch, an educated Dalit man, Ramji Lal Ballai, garlanded Bhanwari and said she was the *mukhiya sadasya* (first citizen) of the village. The main item on the agenda was moving the liquor compound out of the area, something that could be done easily, the sarpanch said, if women petitioned the panchayat.[19] Bhanwari had succeeded in her mission. This cannot be constructed as a "feminist victory", however; at the same time the neighbouring Bassi panchayat honoured the men accused of assaulting Bhanwari, and launched a virulent attack on her and her support groups. Still, the fact that Bhanwari was able to renegotiate social space and dignity for herself, within Bhateri, indicates the potential for feminist interventions.

IV

The story of landless rural Dalit women in Andhra Pradesh who rose up spontaneously, drawing in women from across the state into a struggle that spread like a forest fire bears repetition, for the anti-arrack uprising of 1992 has gone down in the annals of feminist activism as a landmark resistance.

Where and how did the struggle begin? At first sight it appears that its origins were in a literacy programme in Doobagunta, from where it spread throughout the state.[20] The lesson, 'Siripuram Sitamma' in the *Aksharajyoti* primer was the ostensible catalyst; in it, Sitamma, unable to bear the effect of liquor on men, mobilized all the women in her village in order to stop the flow of liquor into it.[21] The imperatives of the struggle, however, go back to something that was simmering much before the literacy programme; this was the growing resistance to an authoritarian and repressive state becoming more and more dependent on the ruling classes. Our concern is with the conditions that enabled women to act at that particular moment in history, inspired by a literacy primer.

The 1980s saw the impoverishment of large sections of the rural and urban poor, with a sharp deterioration in employment, and a 30 to 50 per cent increase in the prices of essential commodities. The government, rather than addressing the question of food subsidies and survival for the poor, introduced new strategies for the maximisation of revenue through a shift in excise policy. The Varuna Vahini programme of the Telugu Desam government, introduced in the early 1980s, was one such. Country-made liquor or arrack, up to that point sold only in bottles, was now available in sachets, making it far easier to transport and consume in greater quantities. The auctioning of liquor vends was centralized at the district level, paving the way for the emergence of a whole class of liquor barons, whose interests in the liquor trade ran into crores of rupees. Individual outlets in villages were then subcontracted to smaller agents who adopted aggressive sale strategies. The nexus between liquor traders and landowners in rural areas made it possible for landlords to pay daily wages in the form of coupons, which could then be exchanged for arrack sachets at liquor shops. Men, in return for a whole day's work, now came home drunk with no money for the family's food.

The anti-arrack movement soon spread to 800 villages, and more than 500 shops were closed down forcibly. Arrack auctions were postponed no less than thirty-two times. Finding that the auctions had no takers, the government decided that the excise department itself would take responsibility for liquor sales. Now the women's struggle was directed against the government. Predictably, the state grew repressive as the struggle spread from one district to another and its financial implications became clear. If allowed to continue unchecked, liquor barons would suffer unprecedented losses. Under pressure from arrack contractors who demanded a refund on their deposits, the Excise Commissioner ordered liquor shops to be re-opened. The police and local toughs were pressed into service to quash the protests. The situation became violent, but the women were undeterred and continued to picket arrack shops and godowns. The government threatened that because state revenue would receive a setback, consequently rations of rice and kerosene would be withdrawn. The women retorted that they could cope with the withdrawal of the rice subsidy, but not with the sale of liquor; they kept forcing more shops to close. When the Jana Vignana Vedika[22] gave a call for a statewide movement, the women devised strategies and action in ways that changed from one moment to the next. They crafted the movement as they went along, experimenting with newer and newer forms of protest. The struggle had already made a difference to women's lives, increasing household savings and providing food to eat. Domestic violence came down drastically—even the men who used to drink habitually acknowledged the change.

The anti-liquor struggle requires us to re-examine the boundaries between the home and the world, between private and public, and our own assumptions regarding the state. Establishing a link between poor rural women and the state machinery at various levels, from local bureaucracies to the head of state, was the hallmark of the struggle. Women experienced at first hand the nature of the ruling class and its relationship to state structures; they now had a new perspective on the violence they were subjected to in their daily lives. They began to recognize and understand that the distinction between private and public is blurred and, in a sense, artificial. "Family issues" were now discussed and debated on the road. The transformation in women's lives was evident from the fact that they were ready to take *collective action* against errant husbands.

The campaigns against domestic violence initiated by feminists in the 1970s now acquired a new relevance. The articulation of family violence in the course of the anti-liquor struggle shifted from a middle-class to a working-class context. In this shift the family acquired a poli-tical centrality and meaning, along with caste and class. Gender relations within the family were reconstituted by the very fact that women sat together publicly not just to discuss problems of survival and domestic violence, but also to talk about how they would deal with men who violated the codes of conduct that women were now laying down.

Further, in fashioning unique forms and strategies of resistance, women redefined the meaning of the political. The struggle was completely decentralized, as was its leadership. Modes of protest, the planning of collective action and decisions regarding the struggle were taken by women at the local level, and the leadership itself was representative of the democratic character of the movement. None of the leaders had a vested interest in it, nor did anyone ask the women to "go home" after the battle was won (or sold out)—as has been the case in many other mass movements across the world with a predominantly male leadership. It is true that what began as a mass movement survives today as token lobbying with a government that sees the entire issue only in terms of revenue. The most important lesson of this decade, however, is the fact of women's agency in devising a prolonged struggle against domestic violence *and* state violence, linking the increase in domestic violence to economic violence by a state in the throes of structural adjustment.

V

A critical part of the effort to re-articulate the issue of caste in the theoretical/political context of anti-racism, has been the mobilizing of Dalit feminist resistance by the National Federation of Dalit Women in India, which began its work in 1995. The manifesto of the NFDW sets it apart from the autonomous women's movement in India on the one hand, and male-dominated secular and progressive movements, including the Dalit movement, on the other; it thus underscores the need for critical reflection on caste-based discrimination *and* the violence inflicted on Dalit women.[23] As set out in its Manifesto,

> The NFDW endeavours to seek and build alliances with all other progressive and democratic movements and forces, in particular the women's movement and the wider Dalit movement, at the national level. It thus aspires in a significant way to widen democratic spaces, while at the same time creating and preserving its identity and specificity.
>
> This framework will enable the Dalit women's movement to seek the roots of its oppression, the diversities, the nature of changes, if any, in specific regions and historical contexts and, in particular, perceive the varied levels of consciousness that exist within it.[24]

This project, while submerged in the larger Dalit mobilization in Durban in 2001, must be examined in greater detail, because it raises questions regarding the relationship between gender and racism as reflective of questions of intersectionality in feminist struggles, even as it examines the specificities of the Dalit woman's question in India. Central to this politics are issues of identity, diversity and power. How has feminism in India fashioned a new politics of identity and belonging that resists sexism and casteism-racism in very direct ways?

In the context of the Durban CERD, Dalit women attempted to combat both racism and sexism, wresting space within the larger Dalit mobilization for a represen-tation of interest and identity *as women,* in opposition to other socially dominant groups within the country and the Indian state on the one hand; and building solidarities with other groups suffering descent-based discrimination in different locales across the world, on the other. The pivotal link was with women of African descent. The recognition of diversity and difference was set against the homogenising practices of majoritarian Hindu nationalism at one level, and the appropriating spaces of showcasing "exotic" Dalit-bahujan cultures and their commodification by the state at another. Deliberations on the Dalit woman's position therefore were based on dignity of labour, cultural expression and democratic politics; the notion of "belonging" for Dalit women was situated firmly within an autonomous space that drew its strength from resistance to appropriation and the building of alliances on equal terms.[25]

In terms of the delineation of issues, the NFDW focussed on the specific interpretation of civil and political rights; the recognition of productive contribution to society in terms of equality, dignity, fair wages, and popular perception; the guarantee of security of person and freedom from the threat of sexual and physical assault; the right to freedom of religion in a context where conversion (in the hope of a better life) resulted in denial of protections and the right to leadership—a claim pitted against non-Dalit men, Dalit men and non-Dalit women. Drawing on the definition of racial discrimination in Article 1 of the CERD, the NFDW asserted that discrimination based on caste is indeed a specific form of racism, intertwined with gender, since Dalit women

> . . . face targetted violence from state actors and powerful

> members of dominant castes and community, especially in the case of rape, mutilation and death; they face discrimination in the payment of unequal wages and gender violence at the workplace that includes fields [as agricultural labourers]; on the streets [as manual scavengers and garbage pickers]; in homes [as domestic workers]; and through religious custom . . .[26]

From being a thrice-oppressed class, Dalit women declare sovereignty and occupy a moral high ground, demonstrating the possibility of being democratic, egalitarian and humane, as well as reaching out to other women's rights movements in a spirit of solidarity. This assertion of a *distinct* identity and simultaneous forging of a *collective* identity in several struggles, marks the Dalit women's movement in very specific ways. The mapping of identity is superimposed on mapping the violence of the caste system and the specific ways in which that violence is gendered—the violence of denial, of degrading work, of religion, of atrocity, of aggression on the Dalit woman's body, of language and of abuse.

The larger questions that are relevant to this debate have to do with the politics of masculinity and misogyny in civil society and women's responses to it; the politics of gender within communities and the resistance to sexism from within; the resistance to sexism and xenophobia in the "national" space by redefining body politics; the demonstration of "better" politics by moving back and forth between the political and the moral, rather than *from* the political *to* the moral. Another useful way of looking at this question is to do so through the lens of social exclusion, thereby contextualising the resistance to it.

These are questions that are immediately relevant to an understanding of the ways in which Dalit women have organized themselves over the past decade in India. Resisting pacific order for Dalit women has been critical to survival, since order for them is based on foundational violence—within the family, in the larger multi-caste communal space, and in the terrain(s) of citizenship(s). The Dalit feminist standpoint, and more specifically the National Federation of Dalit Women, provides a cartography of governance that forces an official reckoning of a new way of seeing.

Conclusion

This chapter has tried to map the diversity of feminist interventions in India over the past decade. The attempt is episodic not exhaustive, but it does indicate the ways in which feminist struggles against violence have addressed a range of intersecting issues; more importantly, it examines the strategies adopted by women's groups to negotiate in those spaces and discourses that have systematically excluded women. Feminism as political practice, for instance, has necessitated a critical engagement between struggles for liberation and pedagogical practice. Popularising the teaching of women's studies and re-inventing curricula in different disciplines has forced universities to contend with radical feminist perspectives and negotiate ways of breaking down the encrustation of patriarchal modes in these institutions of higher learning. The centrality of violence to the experience of caste is something that has not entered the canonical writing of caste in a significant way to date, despite critical contributions by scholars in the last ten years on the interlinkages between caste, gender and violence. The mobilization by the National Federation of Dalit Women reconfigures both the debate on caste within the women's movement, and the debate on feminism in Dalit movements. There have since been several very interesting and engaging studies of caste violence in different regions, basically underscoring the fact that while patriarchy undergirds caste, patriarchy itself is neither homogenous nor equally hegemonic across castes.[27] Yet, as Prem Chowdhry observes from her work on caste and violence in north India, "any infringement of the prescribed codes commonly evokes a violent response".[28] Thus, Bhanwari's struggle to keep the space of the community open to dialogue is an important milestone in sustained feminist activism.

Women's groups across the country have struggled primarily against a state that has either been unresponsive or complicit with families and communities that have divested women of rights with impunity; yet, it has also adopted a feminist rhetoric at times. The Women's Empowerment Policy, 2001, especially, resonates with feminist activism, and women in difficult situations—especially those vulnerable to violence and exploitation—are its central concern. However, this concern, far from being the product of imaginative policy, must be viewed against the corpus of incisive feminist research and sustained advocacy on the entitlement of women to fundamental rights, and resistance to their denial.

Feminist engagements have never been linear or uncritical. Shifts in public and official discourses at a particular historical moment represent a convergence of several forces, not the least of which is critical feminist dialogue with states, governments and communities.

Notes & references

Section I is based on interviews with members of different groups across the country. Supriya Rao interviewed members of Anveshi, MV Foundation, Henry Martyn Institute, AP Women's Network, Prajwala, Sakshi Human Rights Watch, Ankuram, Human Rights Forum, Action Aid-India (Andhra), AIDWA and Consortium of Voluntary Agencies, in Hyderabad, in May 2004.

Bhashwati Sengupta conducted interviews in Guwahati, Calcutta and Bhubaneswar in April-May 2004. In Guwahati, she interviewed Harekrishna Deka, DGP, Assam; Anurita Pathak, North-east Network; and women writers at the Women's WORLD Workshop in Guwahati. In Calcutta she interviewed Bhashwati Chakravorty, *The Telegraph;* Anchita Ghatak and Sanghamitra, Action Aid–West Bengal; and Anuradha Kapoor, Swayam. In Bhubaneswar, she met Asha Hans and Amrita Patel, School of Women's Studies, Utkal University; Supriya Achrekar and Bratindi Jena, Action Aid–Bhubaneswar; Kasturi Mohapatra, Open Learning Systems; and Pramodini Pradhan.

[1] For an in-depth analysis of this, see Ammu Joseph, *Whose News? The Media and Women's Issues* (New Delhi: Penguin, 2006).

[2] The cases discussed here were brought to the Asmita Collective between 2002 and 2004. The names of the survivors have been changed.

[3] Cf. Upendra Baxi, *Liberty and Corruption: The Antulay Case and Beyond* (Lucknow: Eastern Book Company, 1989).

[4] Based on an interview with Supriya Achrekar, Action Aid, April 2004.

[5] A cogent summary of the debates around sex-work and trafficking is available in Rajeswari Sunder Rajan, *The Scandal of the State: Women, Law and Citizenship in Postcolonial India* (New Delhi: Permanent Black, 2003).

[6] Based on an interview with Sanghamitra, May 2004.

[7] Based on an interview with Amrita Patel, April 2004.

[8] Interview with members of Anveshi by Supriya Rao, May 2004.

[9] See the discussion on this point in Chapter 2.

[10] See Chapter 5 for a detailed discussion on this issue.

[11] Report of the Fact Finding Team, 1985 (Hyderabad: Salaha).

[12] Report of the meeting in Bhateri on June 22. "Bhateri Gang Rape: Dateline", Archives of Jagori, Delhi, nd.
[13] Letter to the Home Minister signed by women's organizations from all over the country, dated 4.11.92. Archives of Jagori.
[14] Katherine T. Bartlett, "Feminist Legal Methods", *Harvard Law Review*, 103:4, p. 829, February 1990.
[15] "Bhateri Gang Rape: Dateline", op. cit.
[16] Ibid.
[17] Letter to the Home Minister, quoted earlier, says, "Government doctors, magistrates and other officials were all negligent."
[18] Nirja Misra, Shobhita Rajan, Kavita Srivastava, "The Gang Rape of Bhanwari: Response of State, WDP and Women's Groups", paper presented at the VIth National Conference on Women's Studies, Mysore.
[19] Kavita Srivastava, report of the meeting held on 21.02.95 of the Bhateri panchayat, as told by Bhanwari. Archives of Jagori.
[20] The National Literacy Mission (NLM), one of the five technology missions started by the Rajiv Gandhi government, has taken a different trajectory in each state in the country, determined by local socio-economic conditions and local politics. The government officially launched the NLM in Nellore District on October 2, 1990; the Nellore programme was modelled on the campaign approach, foregrounding issues of development and empowerment, specifically for women, along with enhancing reading and writing skills. The second stage of the mission involved the formation of an academic committee to write the literacy primers; the post-literacy phase saw the establishment of 6,000 Jana Chetana Kendras (Centres for People's Awareness) where women played a key role in addressing and initiating debates on local problems and issues.
[21] The origin of this story was Marripadu in Rambili mandal, where a woman, M. Veerayamma, mobilized women of her village against liquor. This story was included in the primer.
[22] Jana Vignana Vedika is a People's Science Forum which is part of the All India People's Science Network or the BGVS. The aim of the network in different parts of the country has been to mobilize people on the issue of literacy, science and rationality. The National Literacy Mission is an outcome of the work of the BGVS and its state chapters.

[23] See also, Vimal Thorat, "Dalit women have been left behind by the Dalit movement and the women's movement", *Communalism Combat*, May 2001.

[24] *Transforming Pain into Power: The Manifesto of the National Federation of Dalit Women*, nd. National Federation of Dalit Women, Reading Materials of the First National Leadership Training Institute for Dalit Women, Bangalore, November–December 2003. Unpublished. Personal archives of Ruth Manorama.

[25] Ibid.

[26] National Federation of Dalit Women, NGO Declaration on Gender and Racism, Racial Discrimination, Xenophobia and Related Intolerance, World Conference Against Racism, August 28–September 7, 2001, Durban, South Africa. National Federation of Dalit Women, Reading Materials prepared for the National Consultation on Gender and Racial Discrimination, New Delhi, February 2001. Unpublished. Personal archives of Ruth Manorama

[27] Anupama Rao, for instance, argues in favour of caste-specific patriarchies in her essay, "Understanding Sirasgaon: Notes towards Conceptualising the Role of Law, Caste and Gender in a Case of 'Atrocity'", in Rajeswari Sunder Rajan (ed.), *Signposts: Gender Issues in Post-Independence India* (New Delhi: Kali for Women, 1999), p. 208.

[28] Prem Chowdhry, "Enforcing Cultural Codes: Gender and Violence in Northern India", in Mary B. John and Janaki Nair (eds.), *A Question of Silence? Sexual Economies of Modern India* (New Delhi: Kali for Women, 1998), p. 333.

5 Confronting State Violence

Ritu Menon

AN unusual feature of much recent violence in India, sectarian, communal or otherwise, is the documentary reports, testimonies and other evidentiary material that has been produced almost immediately after the event. The 1984 massacre of Sikhs in the wake of Indira Gandhi's assassination was notable for the various citizens' and NGO reports on the complicity of the Congress party, and laxity on the part of law-enforcing agencies in putting an end to the violence. Subsequent years and "riots"—Surat, the Babri Masjid demolition, Antop Hill, the Dangs, among others—have all produced the most damaging accounts of what one analyst refers to as the "post-mortem practices" of the state; in other words, its response to the violence itself and the nature of remedial action taken.[1] Almost without exception, the consensus has been that governments, state and central, have been remiss in discharging their responsibilities towards citizens, and that law-enforcing agencies, like the police and judiciary, have failed in securing justice and redressal for those affected.

Gujarat 2002 marked a new nadir in this phenomenon. The open and unabashed participation of the state government in the genocide against Muslims, post-Godhra, violated every norm of governance and accountability, as well as guarantees of constitutional protection. Indeed, as Upendra Baxi has remarked, state and central complicity in this shameful instance has "ensured that the truth...will never be found, the guilty never punished, and the violated, deprived of rehabilitation, restitution and redress".[2]

In the intervening months and years, several analyses and commentaries on the pathology of Gujarat have appeared, detailing its history (or not) of communal violence, the rise of the BJP and its subsequent Modification.[3] All of these are pertinent to any discussion on violence against women, but this chapter focuses on sexual violence against women by the state and its agents, in Gujarat in 2002, and over the last one decade in Kashmir and Manipur. Although the issue of custodial rape (i.e., rape while under the care and in custody of state agencies and institutions) was one of the first campaigns taken up by the Indian women's movement in its demand for a review of rape laws, it is only recently that attention has been directed towards the increasing sexual violation of women by the state in situations of communal violence and armed conflict. We propose to discuss the case of Gujarat 2002 as an example of the former; and the 2004 rape and murder of a woman militant, Thangjam Manorama, by the armed forces in Manipur, as an all too common example of the latter. Our discussion will also take in similar violence against women in Kashmir and in other parts of north-east India, in an attempt to assess the implications of criminal activity by the state on our conceptualizations of violence against women.

Gujarat, 2002

On February 27, 2002, the Sabarmati Express bound from Godhra to Ahmedabad was allegedly attacked by a "mob" as it pulled out of the station at 8: 05 a.m. According to reports put out by the state government, Muslim "mobs" stoned the train and about half an hour later, one carriage with 58 passengers was burnt to ashes. Among the passengers were many activists of the Vishwa Hindu

Parishad (VHP) returning after a kar seva at the site of the demolished Babri Masjid in Ayodhya.

What followed this gruesome attack on innocent people (for which no one, to date, has claimed responsibility) was unsurpassed in brutality and murderous revenge. For four days, from February 28-March 3, 2002, several districts in Gujarat witnessed the deliberate and blood-curdling murder, arson and looting of Gujarati Muslims and their businesses by angry groups of citizens, hired hoodlums, petty criminals and ambitious local political toughs. More than 2,000 people were killed, hundreds of women raped, mutilated and burnt, and a couple of lakhs driven out of their homes and work places. Terrified and terrorized, they fled to makeshift relief camps set up by NGOs, church and citizens' groups and other civil society organizations, which were completely unable to cope with the thousands of people who sought refuge in them. While the rest of the country reacted with shock and horror to these events, the Gujarat government remained cool in its detachment, calm in its malign neglect.

Even as Narendra Modi's Bharatiya Janta Party (BJP) government shamelessly denied that it had any hand in the violence, the media and independent investigation into the genocide swiftly established its culpability on a number of counts, ranging from dereliction of duty and failure to protect its citizens, to being a co-conspirator in the mass murders. In the face of the state government's refusal to own responsibility for the atrocities that took place between February 28-March 4, citizens' initiatives undertook a detailed documentation of crimes committed; for the purposes of this discussion, however, we will limit ourselves to sexual crimes against women.

Between February 27–March 31, 2002, a six member team of women from Delhi, Bangalore, Tamil Nadu and Ahmedabad—the first such group to visit Gujarat—undertook a fact-finding mission to assess the impact of the continuing violence against Muslim women in the state. They visited seven relief camps in Ahmedabad, Kheda, Vadodara, Sabarkantha and Panchmahals districts, and have said privately that what they saw and heard exceeded their wildest imagination of the worst.[4] The two accounts reproduced below are among the many, many similar stories they were told, some far more horrific than these. The women spoke of being hunted down like quarry, cornered, threatened, brutalized and violated in a nightmare of organized, vengeful violence. The police, they said, stood by and watched.

> On the afternoon of February 28, to escape the violent mob, about 40 of us got on to a tempo wanting to escape to Kalol. My husband Feroze was driving the tempo. Just outside Kalol a Maruti car was blocking the road. A mob was lying in wait. Feroze had to swerve. The tempo overturned. As we got out they started attacking us. People started running in all directions. Some of us ran towards the river. I fell behind as I was carrying my son, Faizan. The men caught me from behind and threw me on the ground. Faizan fell from my arms and started crying. My clothes were ripped off by the men and I was left stark naked. One by one the men raped me. All the while I could hear my son crying. I lost count after three. They then cut my foot with a sharp weapon and left me there in that state.
>
> *Sultani, Kalol Camp, Panchmahals District, March 30, 2002*

The mob started chasing us with burning tyres after we

> were forced to leave Gangotri Society. It was then that they raped many girls. We saw about 8–10 rapes. We saw them strip 16-year-old Mehrunissa. They were stripping themselves and beckoning to the girls. Then they raped them right there on the road. We saw a girl's vagina being slit open. Then they were burnt. Now there is no evidence.
>
> *Kulsum Bibi, Shah e Alam Camp, March 27, 2002*

In a display of absolute and chilling callousness the Gujarat government brusquely dismissed reports of the sexual violation of women, ignoring the gravity of the charges. It denied that large-scale raping and killing had taken place *because the state administration allowed it to* simply by withholding protection, especially to women and children. Slogans like, "*Yeh andar ki baat hai, police hamare saath hai,*" (the police are with us, it's an inside job) were plastered on the walls of gutted Muslim homes. When confronted with the facts, Maya Kodnani, BJP MLA from Naroda Patia where several brutal gang rapes, including of minor girls, had been reported, said, "Is this true? One policeman did mention this to me, but he had not seen anything himself."[5] The District Collector of Panchmahals, whom a women's team interviewed, clearly told them, "Maintaining law and order is my primary concern. It is not possible for me to look into cases of sexual violence. If something is brought to my notice I can take action, but nothing more than that. NGOs should take on this job—I would welcome their involvement."[6]

Harsh Mander of Action Aid, an NGO that was among the first to provide relief assistance in Gujarat, says, "I have never known a riot which has used the sexual subjugation of women *so widely* as an instrument of violence, as in the recent mass barbarity in Gujarat."[7] The operative words here are "so widely", suggesting that the violence was both planned and condoned. Political analyst Achyut Yagnik, writing about the violence that followed L.K. Advani's rath yatra through Gujarat during the Ram Janmabhoomi campaign, noted that for the first time, women and children were seen as legitimate targets of atrocity; the operative word here is "legitimate".[8]

As more than one commentator has pointed out, Modi and the Gujarat government were doing more than denying their culpability—they were asserting their claim to a collective trait in Gujarati Hindus which they called "asmita" or self-esteem; and in asserting it they, at the same time, transformed it into a right and privilege. In the Gujarat carnage, the discourse on Gujarati "asmita"—or what Meghnad Desai calls "bhasmita"—was deployed in all its ghastly aspects. Beginning with the BJP's defence of Narendra Modi's "exemplary" handling of a violent and volatile situation, to the outrageous claim made by some ministers that, but for his timely intervention, many more minority lives would have been lost, we watched and listened with horror as, in Upendra Baxi's words, "The enduring truths of suffering humanity become just so many moments of falsehood in the exercise of practical politics."[9]

In a penetrating analysis of Narendra Modi's appeal to Gujarati "asmita", Baxi notes that it is made up of a blend of "swabhiman/ atmagaurav" (legitimate self and collective pride) and "sahadat" (martyrdom). He goes on to enumerate its other features as enunciated by Modi: religious pluralism and good governance (his example being 75 per cent voter turnout for the state assembly elections in 2002, despite the "kapra" [awful] times they were held in). Modi then declares that instead of "ninda" or condemnation, the nation's honourable men should engage in "pratiksha" (expectation of good governance); and claims that rather than conducting an autopsy, "asmita" offers narratives of a living Gujarat. In this astounding example of doublespeak, Baxi maintains, allegations of massive brutality against women "are represented as libellous of Gujarati multitudes; asmita, translated as a principle of public administration and governance, requires that these stories . . . never be forensically or judicially verified".[10]

This last is critical. The deliberate failure of the police to register cases and to make out the FIRs in such a way as to render complaints un-actionable, has been noted by every single report published or enquiry conducted by NGOs and the National Human Rights Commission (NHRC). The People's Union of Democratic Rights (PUDR) Report notes that the police used tried and tested techniques to falsify records and invalidate charges: unrelated crimes such as arson, stone-pelting, looting and killing in different localities, by different groups, were clubbed together. The official justification was that each violent mob indulged in a range of criminal activity; while this may well be true it made investigation extremely problematic. Another tactic was to distort information in the FIRs, for which the informant was a police officer himself. The scandal in this is obvious: if the police itself is witness to criminal activity but fails to prevent it, how can it be a protective force? Even more serious, however, is the consequence of such falsification when victims themselves approach the police to register an FIR—the existing report serves as an alibi, denying survivors the right to file their own. It also denies them the right to a copy of the FIR, as well as the right to intervene in court during the prosecution.[11] A journalists' team that visited Gujarat in May 2002 and investigated charges of rape was told, "For one attack there can only be one FIR"; a separate FIR for "simply rape" could not be filed because that would be "making a case out of a case".[12] Till the time of writing (January 2005) only *one* rape case had been registered in the whole state.

Underlying this dereliction of duty, however, is a more sinister aspect—that the police was hand in glove with the mobs, often actively participating in the destruction and burning of Muslim shops, houses and vehicles, especially on February 28, 2002, the first day of the carnage. Voters' lists (by which Muslims were identified), arms, gas cylinders and transportation materialized mysteriously. The then state Home Minister, Gordhan Zadaphia, reportedly told former Deputy Superintendent of Police (Bhavnagar), "You are doing a good job, but the ratio of those killed in police firing is not good"—a reference to five Hindus and one Muslim who had been killed in Bhavnagar. Victims repeatedly told social workers that their pleas for protection fell on deaf ears. (*Asian Age*, October 31, 2004) Yet, no action has been taken against the police to date, either disciplinary, departmental or criminal. Dismissals, transfers or suspensions have been non-existent, except of those officers who actually tried to perform their duties.

Following the widespread concern regarding the Gujarat high court's disposal of cases and the petitions in the Supreme Court by the NHRC, the former ordered all cases in the state to be moved out of Gujarat to a neighbouring state. Taking an extremely serious view of the miscarriage of justice in the Best Bakery and other cases (where key witnesses were intimidated by political henchmen of the ruling party), the Supreme Court on November 21, 2003 gave the Modi government two weeks to show cause why 10 major cases in the high court should not be transferred. In case after case all the accused were granted bail, yet the public prosecutor made no objections to this even though the numbers killed were very high.[13] "The conduct of trials," said *amicus curiae* Harish Salve, "in fact, the investigation itself, leaves much to be desired."

In such a climate of fear, flight and intimidation and blatant injustice, it is unlikely that women's complaints will be heard, or indeed, that they will be courageous enough to come forward to register them. Even asking for protection was a hazardous business. Saira Bano, resident of Navapura, Ahmedabad, told Citizens' Initiative that

> The maidan was full of thousands of trishul and sword-wielding men. I have never seen so many people. Everyone was panicking. We lost all hope when the police came with the crowd. When we pleaded with the people that they were meant to protect everyone, they said, "*Tum lad lo. Jitni takat hai mukabla kar lo.*" (You fight them if you have the strength to take them on.)

Testimonies like this were numerous, each more damning of the police than the other. Shabnam, also from Ahmedabad, said,

> The mob arrived armed with swords, shouting, '*Mian ne maro, mian ne kato*! (Kill the Muslims!) We were 50, they

> were a few thousand. As we ran for our lives the police blocked our escape, chasing us in the direction of the mob. '*Chalo, maar do saalon ko*' (Kill the bastards!) they shouted. This is the first time this has happened here. Where can we go? What is to become of us?[14]

On November 25, 2003, almost two years after the carnage, only 12 perpetrators were convicted of crimes committed in February and March of 2002. But, as many activists and lawyers have noted, the immunity of the state remains unassailed—not one officer, policeman or administrator has been indicted for being complicit in murderous violence; moreover, as Elizabeth Jelin has noted, in such situations police action and covert intimidation are "ongoing, systematic and reiterative; the most elementary of civil rights are threatened daily; and minorities face systematic institutional discrimination".[15]

The State Legislative Assembly elections in 2002 returned Narendra Modi to power with a massive majority. Thereafter, the state government, the BJP in Gujarat and at the centre (till May 2004) openly and triumphantly proclaimed its victory, and made no moves at all to address any of the victims' concerns or to ensure their security and safety.

Manipur, 2004

On July 11, 2004, at 3: 30 pm, Havildar Suresh Kumar in Imphal (Manipur) signed a memo stating that he was arresting Thangjam Manorama Devi, 32 years old, "a suspected insurgent, explosives expert and hard core member" of the banned People's Liberation Army (PLA).

Three hours later she was found dead, having been raped and shot in her vagina.

Nearly six kms. from where Manorama's body was found lies Irom Sharmila, who has been on an indefinite fast, refusing to eat a morsel since November 2000, in protest against the Armed Forces (Special Powers) Act, in force in Manipur since 1980. The original anti-AFSPA heroine, she is being kept alive by force-feeding her.[16]

On July 15, four days after Manorama was killed, the entire country was stunned to see photographs in the national press of a most extraordinary protest by women—15 middle-aged women demonstrated naked in front of the gates of Kangla Fort, HQ of the 17 Assam Rifles in Imphal, shouting, "Indian Army, Rape Us!" "Our anger made us shed us our inhibitions that day," said 75 year old Thockchom Ramani, secretary of the Women's Social Reformation and Development Samaj. "If necessary, we will die—commit self-immolation to save our innocent sons and daughters."[17]

For over three months the state of Manipur was in turmoil with frequent strikes, bandhs, protests and demonstrations, demanding that the AFSPA be revoked. Reacting to a spate of custodial and encounter killings, people's anger and resentment flared across the state at the central government's perceived indifference to their demand for punishing the guilty and revoking the AFSPA by August 15, 2004. Strikes and work stoppages were widespread as protesters took to the streets. Activists of the women's group, the Meira Peibis (or Torch-bearers) marched in a candlelight procession through Imphal, and Apunba Lup, an umbrella group of 32 civil and human rights organizations, called for civil disobedience against the AFSPA.[18] Manorama's home became a virtual shrine, uniting activists and ordinary people against the Act.

The reason for their rage is not far to seek. The Armed Forces (Special Powers) Act (1958) grants soldiers legal immunity in a "disturbed" area (which large parts of north-east India have been declared to be) even if they kill someone. Although the Chief Minister of Manipur came under increasingly heavy pressure to withdraw the Act in the weeks that followed Manorama's killing, the Centre remained unmoved. No senior minister visited Imphal, and both Home and Defence Ministers were adamant that the AFSPA would remain in operation. The army was completely opposed to its revocation, saying it would lead to "demoralization" in the armed forces and make for a cascading effect in other states where the Act is in force—notably, Jammu & Kashmir and Assam and Nagaland. Then Defence Minister, Pranab Mukherjee, declared that there was no question of any "rethinking" on the issue; and Home Minister, Shivraj Patil, said that the government would "look into" the feasibility of the demand only "after normalcy returns".[19] A one-man enquiry commission was set up by the state government to investigate the death of Manorama, but events took a rather curious turn hereafter. The Chief Minister of Manipur assured protestors that the Act would be selectively lifted from certain districts in the state; the Union Home Minister contradicted his earlier statement by saying that the Centre was ready to withdraw the Assam Rifles from Manipur: "If this is necessary to restore peace in the area...we are ready to respect the feelings of the people of Manipur"[20]; but the very next day, Defence Minister Pranab Mukherjee categorically stated, "It is not correct to say that there is any move to withdraw the Assam Rifles."[21]

Meanwhile, the Assam Rifles refused to testify before the Commission of Enquiry; the Commanding Officer of 17 Assam Rifles, Col. Jagmohan Singh, and four soldiers known to be present during Manorama's arrest failed to show up at the Commission for four days in succession, claiming that it was "unsafe" for them to testify in open court because of the threat posed by insurgents! (The irony was that the Assam Rifles HQ is situated across the road from the State Guest House where the enquiry was being held.) Yet, cross-examination of the soldiers was vital because of a major discrepancy between the arrest memo handed over to Manorama's family on the night of her arrest, and the seizure memo handed into the Commission by the Army.

On August 28, seven weeks after Manorama was shot by them, the four accused personnel of Assam Rifles appeared before the Commission to depose for the first time. They were brought to its office in a bullet-proof jeep, surrounded by armed personnel;[22] on September 16 the Chief of Army Staff, General N.C. Vij, told news reporters in Srinagar that Manorama was a woman of "questionable credentials" and that she had not been raped by his soldiers.[23] Up until the time of writing the Commission of Enquiry investigating Manorama's killing had met with no success. The Army refused to release its forensic report on DNA samples taken from the accused, and the Manipur government likewise, has refrained from releasing its report to the Army. In a major concession to popular sentiment and state compulsions, the central government finally handed over Kangla Fort to the Government of Manipur on November 20, 2004.

I

Independent India enacted several pieces of legislation after the British left, among them the Assam Maintenance Public Order (Autonomous Districts) Act of 1953, the Assam Disturbed Areas Act of 1955, the Armed Forces (Assam and Manipur) Special Powers Act of 1958, and the Armed Forces (Special Powers) Act of 1972. Though the AFSPA has its antecedents in British India, there are significant differences between the British and Indian acts. The British granted special powers only to a commissioned officer, not below the rank of a captain in the army; by contrast, the Indian AFSPA grants this power to all security personnel, irrespective of their rank: they can shoot anyone merely on the basis of suspicion.

The major act governing military action in the north-east of India and in Jammu & Kashmir is the Armed Forces (Special Powers) Act of 1958 and 1972. It is intended specifically for use in "disturbed areas", though no precise definition of such an area is given. The Act has been in force in the whole of Nagaland since 1995; in selected districts (those characterized as "insurgent") of Manipur since 1980; and in the Kashmir Valley since 1989–90. First enacted in 1958 to deal with rebellion in Assam and Manipur, it was extended in 1972 to cover all five states and two Union Territories of the North-east (Assam, Manipur, Tripura, Nagaland, Mizoram, Arunachal Pradesh and Meghalaya.) Since Independence, security forces—consisting of the army, air force, paramilitary forces and special operations groups—have been deployed on a more or less constant basis in the North-east; some estimates claim that, numerically, there is one security personnel for every 10 civilians in the region.[24] Manipur alone currently has 13 battalions

(10,000 men) of the Assam Rifles, four battalions of the army, and eight battalions of the Central Reserve Police Force in the state, as well as state security forces like the Manipur Rifles. Since the 1980s, when most of these battalions were deployed, insurgency has been unabated, and hundreds of "insurgents" and "hard core members" of barred outfits have been killed in questionable circumstances.

Of all the Acts legislated by the Indian government to curb extremism or militancy, the AFSPA is probably the most draconian in its provisions. It grants unrestricted and unaccountable powers to the security forces. The Enforcement Section (4) of the Act, for instance, gives members of the armed forces, down to the rank of non-commissioned officer, the power to shoot and kill, to enter and search, and to arrest without warrant any person against whom there is a reasonable suspicion of either having committed, or intending to commit, a cognizable offence. The "disturbed area" classification makes it mandatory for any person who wants to institute legal proceedings against injustice(s) perpetrated on him/her under the AFSPA to seek—according to Section 6—the prior sanction of the central government. *The construction of this section makes it almost impossible for anyone to seek redress for grievances or legal protection against violation(s) of fundamental right(s).* Provisions in Section 4 and 6 meanwhile, provide security personnel with legal immunity for actions in aid of maintaining law and order; and "in aid to civil power". The Indian parliament has enforced this law for indefinite periods, without review, in large parts of the northeastern region.[25]

The history of military occupation and the use of the

armed forces to contain civil unrest is replete with instances of abuse, uncalled for violence and human rights violations. The Indian experience in Kashmir and the North-east is no exception to this, and the protracted nature of insurgency in these regions has exacerbated the situation as violence begins to replicate itself. In low-intensity conflict, armies use counter-insurgency tactics designed to destroy infrastructure. Security personnel conduct body searches, storm homes at night on the pretext of search and seizure, hold families of suspected militants hostage, and otherwise intimidate and humiliate women. Sexual abuse is more the rule than the exception. In Kashmir—which has an estimated 500,000 soldiers, paramilitary and police fighting approximately 3,000 militants—the number of dead are reported at 50,000, and of widows, about 30–40,000.[26] In addition there are between 3,000–8,000 "missing" persons and their "half-widows".

Based on court martial statistics provided by the army, it has received 1426 complaints of human rights violations over the last one decade; it court-martialled 50 men, dismissed 17 in the NE and punished 61 soldiers in Kashmir.[27] A human rights report on Kashmir alone for 1996 documented 13,000 cases of molestation in the years since the army crackdown.[28] The infamous Bijbehara, Malangaon and Kunan-Poshpora rapes in 1991, widely protested by women's groups and the subject of a special investigation by the Press Council of India, detailed the extent and occurrence of sexual abuse by the security forces in Kashmir.[29]

In Nagaland, the roster of sexual crimes against women stretches back to the mid-1950s. In 1960, A.Z. Phizo submitted an appeal to the United Nations in which he enumerated dozens of cases of sexual violation by the armed forces and security personnel, between 1954–1957. They included the full repertoire of violence from rape and mutilation to rubbing chilli powder into women's genitals; forcible fondling, kissing and biting; stripping and flogging; beating pregnant women's stomachs with boots and rifle butts; brutally raping minor girls; gang-raping; and of course, killing in the presence of family members.[30] A WISCOMP team that visited the districts of Wokha, Zunheboto, Mokokchung, Dimapur and Kohima in 2000 corroborated the ghastly Yaukeli Baptist Church rape of four young girls (aged 17, 15, 12 and 11 years) in the church pulpit in 1971, by officers of the First Maratha Regiment (Eighth Mountain Division). It also confirmed the Akuluto firing incident of 1995; the Mokokchung firing and arson incident of 1994; and several others, in all of which women were sexually violated by the armed forces.[31]

The immunity granted to security and armed personnel under the AFSPA has meant that they are not liable for any criminal act committed in the line of "duty". Over the decades that they have been deployed in the Northeast and Jammu & Kashmir, the armed forces have been accused of repeated encounter killings, torture, disappearances and the brutal repression of insurgents and their families. (In Manipur alone, more than 18 such killings were reported in the first few months of 2004.) Women and young girls, and female members of insurgents' families are especially vulnerable, often deliberately targetted by the forces in their attempt to extract information on militant activity. Sexual violation, then, is a common weapon, commonly used. However, it would be hard to justify such a violation of women as being necessary either to the maintenance of law and order or to the curbing of "terrorism"; so the authorities have done the next best thing—denied that any such offence ever took place. As did General Vij in the rape and killing of Manorama Devi, although the court martial instituted by the Assam Rifles claimed that four of its personnel had been kept in confinement. Human rights lawyer, Nandita Haksar, who worked with civil society organizations in the North-east during the 1980s and '90s, cited the 1987 Oinam counter-insurgency operation in which two pregnant women were forced to deliver their babies in a school playground, surrounded by jawans.

> We presented 10,000 pages of evidence of atrocities committed by security forces during the Oinam operations . . . but till today (2004) there has been no judgement. . . Where is the space for justice for the people of the North-east?[32]

In the case of the Kunan-Poshpora rapes of 1991 in Kashmir, an elaborate investigation by the Press Council of India came to the conclusion that

> . . . the evidence offered, whether directly to us or through earlier news accounts, simply does not add up. It is riddled with contradictions of the most elementary kind. We concur with the Divisional Commissioner's finding that the so-called incident has been grossly exaggerated.[33]

The repeated failure of the central government to check this scandalous abuse of power not only perpetuates violence, it seriously vitiates the state government's authority and capacity to deal with excesses. In the case of Assam Rifles, for instance, the latter virtually took over the district of Oinam in Nagaland in 1971, ran a parallel administration, and forbade the then chief minister from visiting the area.[34] In the aftermath of Thangjam Manorama's killing in 2004, the state government took the extraordinary step of defying the central government and withdrawing the AFSPA from selected parts of Imphal before the August 15 deadline.

II

The all-women's group, the Meira Peibis, has been one of the most important social organizations in Manipur to resist a wide range of social ills. It was formed initially to mobilize women against alcoholism and rowdyism among Manipuri men, but it has since extended its activities to take in other social issues, especially the increasing militarization of the state. Among other things, the Meira Peibis have consistently opposed the AFSPA; they have demonstrated, fasted, held protest meetings and systematically brought abuses by the armed forces to public notice. They have taken up rape cases and volunteered legal help; they have even mediated with the army on occasion, and organized public meetings with them,[35] and they have intervened between civil society and underground groups. "Soldiers in Sarong(s)", a film made on the Meira Peibis, powerfully communicates the steady resolve of the women in the face of recurrent brutality by the armed forces, culminating in a damning list of women raped by them since the1980s. These are ordinary women, by no means radical or even subversive, yet they remain undeterred in their demand for the withdrawal of the AFSPA from Manipur. Notwithstanding this history of resistance, the naked protest by

15 women at the gates of Kangla Fort on July 15 was unprecedented, both as a statement of outrage and for what it signified.

The range of protests that women have used in situations of armed conflict and violence have varied in form and content, from conventional demonstrations and rallies to vows of silence, hunger strikes and the more extreme fasts unto death. Unconventionally, women have also protested and marked their resistance in more individual and symbolic ways by, for instance, refusing to change out of the clothes they were wearing when abducted in the aftermath of the Partition of India;[36] or wearing their hair loose during the entire period of mourning for their slain husbands and menfolk, in the wake of Indira Gandhi's assassination in 1984. Veena Das quotes the widows of Sultanpuri as saying:

> They have asked us to clean up our houses and to go in and settle down. How can we settle down here? Do you see the heaps of ashes? Do you see the blood? Here, put your hand inside this heap and you will see the melted skulls. They would not even let us have the dead bodies. We begged them—you have killed our men, let us have their bodies at least, let us mourn them properly.

Not only did the women make their mourning public, they "defiantly hung on to their filth and their pollution. They would not go into their houses, they would not light the hearth, and they would not change their clothes."[37] In other words, they refused to return to normalcy, to resume their daily lives.

In more collective forms of resistance, and in protest against the disappearance of their sons, mothers in Sri

Lanka and Kashmir have asserted motherhood in order to shame the authorities into recognizing their status as wronged mothers, demanding information on their children's whereabouts. Parveena Ahangar's search for her missing son in Kashmir eventually led to the formation of the Association of the Parents of Disappeared Persons (APDP) and to a cry for collective justice. The refusal of the women of Kunan-Poshpora to remain silent about their rapes by the Indian security forces led to the highlighting of military atrocities; the public cursing of the Mothers' Front in Sri Lanka forced the government into acknowledging its role in the disappearance of thousands of young JVPers; the Women in Black, the Madres of the Plaza de Mayo, the Jaffna Mothers' Front took their private sorrow and made it public, thereby not only radicalising the personal, radicalising even motherhood, but shaming the institutional and authoritarian. As Elizabeth Jelin says of the women's protests in the Southern Cone of South America, "Mothers, relatives, grandmothers and widows erupted in the public arena as bearers of the social memory of human rights violations."[38]

But the July 15, 2004 protest by 15 Meitei women was a radically, and profoundly, different kind of challenge to the state, and in sharp and shocking contrast to Irom Sharmila's four year fast against the AFSPA. Sharmila's protest, like other fasts unto death, offers up her own body in the cause of justice; the Meitei women, on the other hand, publicly presented their naked bodies as a rebuke—"Indian Army, rape us!" they shouted, challenging the authorities by drawing graphic attention to the shameful violation of women's bodies by them. By saying, "We are Manorama's mothers," they as good as declared that her rape was tantamount to raping them, and by extension, *all* Manipuri women and *all* mothers. As sacrilege, the rape of the mother is the most unpardonable violation, yet the 15 women exposed their naked bodies as the ultimate in self-abnegation, and in symbolic recognition of the threat of rape as the power of all men over all women. At another level, however, their protest redefined the hitherto unbridgeable distance between the armed forces and the citizenry by forcing the attention of both upon themselves.

III

The privilege of immunity has always been granted to the armed forces and to law, order and security personnel of the state, on grounds of discharging their duty in the service of society and in the interests of national security. Long before legislation like the AFSPA of 1958, or the Prevention of Terrorism Act (2002) and the Terrorism and Disruptive Activities Act (1985) were passed, the Indian government had enacted the Abducted Persons (Recovery and Restoration) Act in 1949, and the Displaced Persons (Claims) Act in 1950, in addition to sundry ordinances that dealt with refugee resettlement and compensation. Other clauses and sections in these Acts apart, the indemnity clauses in both are strikingly similar to those in the AFSPA. Clauses 10 & 11 of the Displaced Persons (Claims) Act provide that:

1. No Civil Court shall have jurisdiction in respect of any matter which the Chief Claims Commissioner or the Claims Officer is empowered by or under this Act, to determine, and no injunction shall be granted by any

court or other authority in respect of any action taken or to be taken in pursuance of any power conferred by or under this Act.

2. *Protection of action taken in good faith*—No suit, prosecution or other legal proceeding shall lie against the Central Government or any person appointed under this Act in respect of anything which is in good faith done, or intended to be done, in pursuance of this Act or of any rules or orders made thereunder.[39]

The chief claims commissioner was also empowered to delegate all or any of his powers under the Act to any claims commissioner or joint or chief claims commissioners, if he so decided. The central government, in turn, reserved the right to determine the form and manner in which claims could be submitted; the levy of fee in respect of claims submitted; the manner in which claims could be registered; and the manner in which inquiries were held by any or all of the claims officers, commissioners or their deputies. The most critical provision of this Act, however, was that no appeal against decisions could be entertained unless cleared by the chief claims commissioner.

Members of the Legislative Assembly, while debating this Act, pleaded for an amendment that would enable appeals "on certain specific grounds" to be allowed "as a matter of right", but they were turned down. Shri Mohan Lal Saksena, Minister of State for Rehabilitation, clarified that appeals could also be entertained through application by the aggrieved person, but he said, "We do not want to give the right to appeal *as a matter of course* . . . because if we do so then in each and every case there will be an appeal." The amendment was rejected.[40]

The Abducted Persons Act, clause 4, sections 1 & 2 stated that:

1. If any police officer, not below the rank of an Assistant Sub-Inspector or any other police officer specially authorized by the Provincial Government in this behalf, has reasons to believe that an abducted person resides or is to be found in any place, he may, after recording the reasons for his belief, without warrant, enter and search the place and take into custody any person found therein who, in his opinion, is an abducted person, and deliver or cause such person to be delivered to the custody of the officer in charge of the nearest camp with the least possible delay.
2. In exercising any powers conferred by sub-section (1) any such police officer may take such steps and may require the assistance of such female persons as may, in his opinion, be necessary for the effective exercise of such power.

And clause 9 provided that:

> No suit, prosecution or other legal proceedings whatsoever shall lie against the Central Government, the Provincial Government or any officer or authority for, or in respect of, any act which is in good faith done, or intended to be done, in pursuance of this Act.

The state justified the extraordinary powers vested in the police by claiming that it was acting as "the responsible government of a civilized society",[41] in the women's interest, and on behalf of their families—the state as *mai-baap*, or *pater familias.* The suspension of their fundamental rights as citizens was therefore not at issue. The tactics and strategies used by the police or armed forces for cordon and search, or search and seizure, are the same whether they are recovering an abducted woman or "flushing out" militants. Both are hunted down in the same way and both, curiously enough, are considered to be acting against the national interest in their resistance.

In the decades since Independence, successive Indian governments and the Indian state have routinely dismissed allegations of human rights violations as a "hue and cry" raised by human rights organizations, "because they don't know what the ground reality is".[42] They have claimed extraordinary circumstances, violent hostility, armed attack and pre-emptive strikes as extenuating considerations, implying that it is they, rather than the insurgents, who are at the receiving end of hit-and-run violence. An unofficial tally of human rights violations by the armed forces in Jammu & Kashmir and in the North-east over the 10 year period, 1993–2004, is instructive. Of the 1385 allegations received in Jammu & Kashmir, 1349 were investigated; 1316 were found baseless; 33 found true; and 36 were under investigation. Of the 451 received in the North-east, 426 were investigated; 398 were found baseless; 28 found true; and 25 were being investigated. Of the cases found "true", 48 per cent were cases of violations against women in Jammu & Kashmir; and in the North-east, they were 57 per cent.[43]

In the Kunan-Poshpora case in Kashmir, the allegation was that a mass rape of women was committed by men of the 4th Rajputana Rifles of the 68 Mountain Brigade during a cordon and search operation, in Kupwara district. The women—not less than 23 but possibly as many as 100—were of all ages and conditions: pregnant, deaf-mute, retarded and elderly, and the charges were that they were raped by one to seven men at a time, from 11: 00 p.m. to 4: 00 a.m. on the night of February 23/24, 1991. The soldiers were said to be drunk, and the commanding officer and eight other commissioned officers busy at a couple of interrogation centres.[44] According to the army its column moved away from the village at 9: 00 a.m., the operation concluded, after having procured a no-objection certificate from three "village notables" and two police constables who had accompanied the troops.

After an FIR was filed by the women and they were sent for a medical examination, the medical report submitted by the PHC (Kralpura) on the women mentioned "abrasions on their chests and abdomens, on their lips, on both sides of the face, and on arms, legs and different parts of their bodies;" but because they were examined 20 days after the alleged molestation, there could be no conclusive "proof" of rape. Nevertheless, the Note by the medical officer mentioned that the hymens of three "vargins" (sic), 15 and 16 years old, "were found torn".[45] Both the army and the Press Council dismissed the allegations as a complete fabrication. The Council concluded that

> The so-called incident has . . . been grossly exaggerated. . . The Committee's own visit to Kunan-Poshpora and its meeting with the *dramatis personae* gives the lie to the cassette which provides conclusive evidence that the video recording was a carefully rehearsed piece of disinformation . . . made and marketed to arouse anger and hatred among viewers unacquainted with the facts; to intensify alienation, and win external sympathy. . .
>
> The Kunan rape story stands totally unproven and

completely untrue, a dirty trick to frame the Army and get it to lay off Kunan-Poshpora.[46]

The Army itself could not have done better to exonerate itself.

IV

The occurrence of what is euphemistically called the "exploitation" of women in regions under military occupation places the security and armed forces, as well as the state/government in an uncomfortable situation. As mentioned earlier, sexual violence against women by agents of the state can by no means be justified as being necessary to maintaining law or order, curbing "terrorism", or in the national interest. Predictably, the most common response by the state has been to deny that it takes place at all. This is becoming increasingly difficult, however, as the media and independent investigations by a range of civil society organizations and human rights commissions have begun systematically documenting and exposing such abuses. When the evidence against them builds up and pressure mounts then, as we have seen in both Gujarat and Manipur (and also in Jammu & Kashmir and other parts of the North-east), the tendency is to subvert due process and stymie the investigations through inaction, stone-walling and refusal to comply by the police, the administration and the security forces. All these have been deployed unfailingly, most reprehensibly by the Gujarat government, to the extent that even judicial proceedings have been seriously jeopardised.

But it is the "women's question" that most sharply

highlights the conundrum of the state as protector/ perpetrator, and this throws up some important issues for consideration. A senior army officer in Jammu & Kashmir told us (on condition of anonymity) that,

> Exploitation (read rape) of women occurs because of vendetta. Therefore a soldier would have no reason to do it as personal grievances don't come into play. However, when these do occur, the army does not put it into the public domain for two reasons: one, because the soldier has been punished already, been court-martialled by the army; two, because it may cause embarrassment to the women. Instead, the army ensures the rehabilitation of women who have been raped or molested.

Punishment, he said, includes termination of services, administrative and disciplinary action, and life imprisonment.

In an interview with the journalist, Sukhmani Singh, in October 1990, the then Director General of Police (Jammu & Kashmir), J.N. Saksena, admitted to "excesses" by security forces in the Valley. In response to a question regarding the number of rape cases taken up by the authorities he said,

> We have 32 cases of criminal offence so far, of which four are those of rape and two of attempt to rape. In the case of the . . . rape of the bride in Anantnag district, all the jawans involved have been suspended.[47]

When asked why the maximum number of rapes and atrocities had taken place in Kupwara district, he replied, "Because it is a badly infested area." When asked about the eight rapes registered in Pazipora alone, he replied:

> Whenever we have credible information we have taken up the case. In fact, they sent us a list of 14 girls but all these allegations were made two days after the incidents occurred. . . In addition, a large number of senior officers were present that day so it was not possible that so many rapes had taken place. We picked out only those we were convinced were genuine.
>
> . . . I agree there have been aberrations, we are trying to see that *they are reduced to the minimum* (emphasis added)[48]

The army's official response to Singh's report however, was to declare that

> The Armed Forces epitomize the secular fabric of our nation, where caste, creed and religion have no relevance in the execution of their functions. Notwithstanding some occasional aberrations, their discipline is a matter of pride, more particularly where this is becoming more and more fragile in the society around us. The intelligentsia and the media therefore, have a major role to play in helping the soldier to undertake his allotted tasks with dignity and pride.[49]

In a similar vein, in the matter of Manorama Devi's murder, General Vij denied that she had been raped, at the same time as an internal enquiry by the armed forces admitted that "lapses" had occurred.

These contradictory statements ("we never do, but if we do..."), rare in themselves, enable us to examine some significant aspects of sexual violence against women by the state. The first is a tacit (but unacknowledged) acceptance that the sexual violation of women, even by agents of the state, is only to be expected when insurgency, communal violence and armed conflict occur. The rhetoric of denial and denunciation thus takes place *at the same time as the violation,* and the two are neither inconsistent nor irreconcilable. Moreover, the simultaneity of both helps in normalizing such violence, as well as in ensuring a kind of social silence around it. Women's silence can usually be taken for granted ("women themselves have not complained," said our army officer) for all the well-known reasons, but society's complicity is also desirable if the public denunciation is to have any credibility at all. At the same time, the state cannot afford to be seen as being guilty of criminal assault; so extenuating circumstances, stress and hardship; and human (read male) frailty are put out as explanations for the rare instances of "aberrant" behaviour. The Press Council Report, quoted earlier, says:

> It is not the Army's contention that its men can do no wrong. It admits that excesses may be committed in isolated cases, but is quick to point out that supervision is so close . . . and standards of discipline so exacting, that any default . . . if proven, is swiftly punished.[50]

The difficult circumstances in which the forces operate may make for lapses, and these lapses crave our indulgence. In any case, as ex-Defence Minister, George Fernandes, said of the Gujarat cases, it's only a rape, why make such a fuss about it? As with torture and other brutal tactics, rape, too, can be countenanced as being part of "counter-insurgency" measures. In other words, in times of conflict and in "disturbed" areas, a blind eye may be turned to what in "normal" times would be unpardonable. Thus we see that at the same time that the state normalizes its own violence against women, it also exempts itself from criminal liability. We recall that this immunity already exists through the terms of the various legislations enacted; what is significant is that now social sanction is sought for the state's culpability through the motions of simultaneous denial and admission.

In the case of the Gujarat violence of 2002, however, even this equivocation was absent.

V

The "male" in the state: what it means for women

> *All these stories being told to us, one by one, as if this is the first time this country has heard these stories—where a mother is killed and the foetus taken out of her stomach; where a daughter is raped in front of her mother; of someone being burnt…is this the first time such things have happened?*
>
> —Ex-Defence Minister, George Fernandes, defending the BJP government in Parliament during the debate on Gujarat, April 30, 2002

The abiding image from the film, "Soldiers in Sarong(s)" is of the torch-bearing Meira Peibis, the human and female face of a militarized state on one side, and of the military "in full display of their masculinity", on the other.[51] (The photograph of Meitei women protesting in front of the Army HQ in Imphal is in stark contrast to the much more common images of the violated female body.) Men dominate the institutional aspects and structures of conflict; women, children and "feminized" men, its dominated Other. Repression itself, as Jelin eloquently elaborates, is gendered, carried out "by masculine and patriarchal institutions—the armed forces and the police".[52] Rituals of power in the public sphere, she says, "unambiguously stage the opposition between the active/empowered masculine subject and the passive/excluded feminized audience, an audience that may at times, involve the entire civilian population". Personalised symbols of pain and suffering tend to be "embodied in women, while . . . repressive mechanisms appear to 'belong' to men". The teenage face of Zahira Sheikh, her pigtails framing it on either side, has almost become synonymous with the Gujarat massacres, just as the predominant images from Kashmir, whether of militants or the armed forces, are those of violent armed confrontation. (Symbolically, the female figure here is usually the veiled woman.) Counterposed against the fear-inducing and power regalia of the armed forces—the uniforms, the weaponry, the parades and patrols—are the feminine objects of resistance used by women—candles, flowers, scarves and diapers, and photographs.[53]

The female body has always been a special object in regimes of torture and repression, and especially so in instances of ethnicised or communalized violence. Experiences of these several forms of violence are sharply gendered, and they remain so even at the hands of the state. The patriarchal (or Male) state endorses male "ownership" of women, an ownership that manifests itself unabashedly in inter-community violence. It is tacitly agreed that the state and its agencies will move to control this tendency if it erupts into criminal assault and violation; in the Gujarat carnage of 2002, however, the state government and administration actively assisted and participated in the violence against Muslims, and Muslim women and children, abstained from controlling it, denied that it had been orchestrated, desisted from providing relief and rehabilitation and, in many instances, aided and abetted in the intimidation of victims. In other words, far from being protector, it became perpetrator; and the violence, far from being communal, was genocidal.

In the context of insurgency or armed civilian conflict, as in Kashmir and the North-east, the state and its agents engage in "legitimate" violence against mutinous citizens, among them women who are caught in the crossfire. These are the unintended victims; but there are also those women who are targetted either because they are a direct threat themselves, like Thangjam Manorama, or because they are a conduit to insurgent males. In such cases, the unstated but implicit intention is to intimidate, humiliate and even criminally assault if necessary, in order to apprehend the "enemy". Sexual violence against women by the state then, is not only criminal and genocidal, it shares prevailing social and psychological prejudices and becomes *communalized* and *ethnicized*, as indicated by our discussion of the violence in Gujarat, Manipur and Kashmir. Tanika Sarkar has analysed the revenge and hate-filled sexual brutalization of Muslim women's and girls' bodies during the carnage in Gujarat; linking it to an old and induced anxiety about Hindu male "impotence" in the face of unbridled Muslim male "virility" and Muslim female "overfertility". At the time, the Gujarat state general secretary of the VHP signed leaflets that included a shameful poem which boasted disgusting sexual intent:

We have untied the penises that were tied till now
We have widened the tight vaginas of the bibis.[54]

The state government assented silently. A criminal state then uses a devious insider/outsider rhetoric (L.K.Advani, Union Home Minister in 2002, told journalists that the "needle of suspicion" pointed towards the Inter Services Intelligence unit in Pakistan for the train massacre), followed up by threats to justify its actions in the case of communalized violence. Narendra Modi, in a televised statement on February 28, 2002 said: "We will set an example that nobody, not even in his dreams, thinks of committing a heinous crime like this."[55] In ethnicized violence against its citizens, the state summons up the incontestable logic of national security to grant itself immunity from judicial action. Through a combination of administrative and executive inaction and dissembling (what Upendra Baxi calls "democidal governance") and legal immunity, a criminal state seeks to become a state above the law by so contriving events and evidence that there can be no real hope of justice for the dead or brutalized.

For our analysis of state sexual violence against women, two of Wendy Brown's four modalities of contemporary state power are especially relevant. In addition to its capitalist and juridical-legislative or liberal dimensions, as mentioned earlier, she has identified the prerogative dimension, the state's "legitimate arbitrary power in policy making, and legitimate monopolies of internal and external violence in the police and military"; and, second, the bureaucratic dimension, one of the voices of the "organizational structure of state processes and activities". She argues that these two dimensions, in particular, actually produce state subjects as powerless victims, so that to claim rights or redressal, then, becomes a cruel hoax.[56] In her discussion of the prerogative dimension, she cites Machiavelli as the one political thinker who most extensively treated the dynamics and configurations of prerogative power—"its heavily *extra legal*, adventurous, violent and sexual characteristics". According to Brown, he "theorizes political power in a register in which violence, sexuality and political purpose are thoroughly entwined". She then refers to Max Weber's tale of the origins of the state, in which the first set of origins "features a combination of predatory sexuality, territoriality, violence and brotherhood in warrior league activity".

Gujarat 2002 exemplified Brown's second modality, the bureaucratic dimension, in an obvious illustration; but it went far beyond any bureaucratic acts of omission and commission. According to Baxi, Gujarat 2002 brazenly abandoned any attempt at concealing its predilection for what he calls "rape culture" which, he says,

> . . . signifies ways of doing party politics and managing governance in which brutal collective sexual assaults on women *remain enclosed in contrived and escalating orders of impunity* (emphasis mine). In an operative rape culture, then, women's right to *be* and *remain* human depends not on the normative necessity of law or constitution, but on the contingent necessities of the politics of fraud and force. Rape culture names violence against women as a situation of *misfortune*, not as an act of *injustice*.

Or as a criminal offence. Baxi maintains that this tolerance of sexual crimes against women is intrinsic to such a culture. He says

> . . . it affects all state agencies and forms of articulation of state power, although it manifests differently, depending on the authority and auspices. Gujarat 2002 thus presents an extraordinary spectacle in which the National Commission for Women, in a much belated 'investigation', sanitises, through unfeeling prose, violence and violation of women. The relatively more engaged prose of the National Commission of Human Rights' preliminary report is indeed exemplary but provides no real strategies against rape culture. Similarly, the vaunted judicial activism suffers a quietus: neither the High Court of Gujarat nor the Supreme Court of India, on their own (*suo motu*) summon the state advocate general and the attorney general of India to assist judicial invigilation of active law enforcement for the violated women. In this situation, police and prosecutorial agencies remain complicitly lackadaisical.[57]

Brown elaborates this further and extends her argument by asserting that

> The masculinism of state prerogative power inheres in both its violent and its transcendent features. . . Because prerogative power appears to its subjects as not just the power to violate but also the power to protect—quintessentially, the power of the police—it is quite difficult to challenge from a feminist perspective.[58]

What consequences does this implication of the state in sexual violence against women have on our theory and practice? If a "masculine" state (to use Catherine MacKinnon's characterization) subscribes to and endorses society's patriarchal attitudes; if its laws and regulatory mechanisms and procedures are inherently gendered; if it finds itself either normalizing or naturalizing a range of discriminatory and derogatory practices; if it does little to actively dismantle structural inequalities and institutionalized violence; if, in the matter of sexual violence against women, it is also participant and perpetrator, then the state-society divide begins to blur. The state as agent of social change pitted against "recalcitrant, backward, poor and illiterate" society begins to recede; the state as guarantor of non-discrimination and upholder of fundamental rights and constitutional guarantees of equality is compromised; and as protector of citizens' security and safety it has been negligent, at best; often complicit, communal and culpable; and, at worst, even "democidal".

Yet, difficult and contradictory though it may be to deal with them, neither state institutions nor judicial remedies can be dispensed with. Rather than dismantling state structures, it might be more constructive to work towards removing the "Male" in the state, even if this entails recasting it entirely.

Notes & references

[1] Upendra Baxi, "The Gujarat Catastrophe: Notes on Reading Politics as Democidal Rape Culture", in Kalpana Kannabiran (ed.), *The Violence of Normal Times: Essays on Women's Lived Realities* (New Delhi: Women Unlimited, 2005).

[2] Ibid., p. 332.

[3] In this ocean of material see, especially, Syeda S. Hameed, et al, *The Survivors Speak*, Report of a Fact-finding by a Women's Panel (New Delhi: 2002); *Seminar: Society Under Siege*, May 2002; Tanika Sarkar, "Semiotics of Terror: Muslim Children and Women in Hindu Rashtra", *Economic and Political Weekly*, July 13, 2002; Self-Employed Women's Association, *Shanti Path: Our Road to Restoring Peace* (Ahmedabad, 2002); Muchkund Dubey and Syeda S. Hameed, *Gujarat: Four Months Down the Road*, A Report for the Fraternity and Reconciliation Forum, July 2002; Kamal Mitra Chenoy, et al, *Gujarat Carnage, 2002: A Report to the Nation*; People's Union for Democratic Rights, *Gujarat Genocide, Act Two: Six Months Later* (Delhi: September 2002); *Communalism Combat*, "Gujarat—One Year Later", April 2003; Satish Deshpande, "Between Jhatka and Halal: Gujarat After Two Years of 'Normalcy'", *Himal South Asia* (Kathmandu: March-April, 2004); and sundry reports, essays, papers and documents.

[4] *The Survivors Speak*, op. cit.

[5] Ibid., p. 3.

[6] Ibid., p. 4.

[7] Harsh Mander, "Cry, the Beloved Country: Reflections on the Gujarat Massacre", unpublished report circulated on the Internet, March 21, 2002.

[8] Quoted in Ashis Nandy, "Obituary of a Culture", *Seminar*, op. cit., p. 17.

[9] Upendra Baxi, op. cit., and "Notes on Holocaustian Politics," *Seminar*, op. cit.

[10] Upendra Baxi, "The Gujarat Catastrophe", op. cit., pp. 345–348.

[11] A detailed account of this obstruction of justice is available in the PUDR Report, *"Maaro! Kaapo! Baalo!": State, Society and Communalism in Gujarat* (Delhi: May 2002), pp. 34–39.

[12] Barkha Dutt in *Outlook*, May 2002.

[13] Report in *The Indian Express*, November 22, 2003.

[14] *The Survivors Speak*, op. cit., pp. 18–20.

[15] Elizabeth Jelin, *State Repression and the Labours of Memory* (Minneapolis: University of Minnesota Press, 2003), p. xvi.

[16] Reported in *The Indian Express*, August 1, 2004. In September-October 2006, she was brought to the capital, Delhi, and hospitalised against her wishes.

[17] Reported in *Tehelka*, August 7, 2004.

[18] *The Indian Express*, August 10, 2004.

[19] Sundry newspaper reports followed the progress of this debate as it unfolded; what is presented here is a composite version of those reports.

[20] *The Hindu*, August 10, 2004.

[21] *The Times of India*, August 11, 2004.

[22] *The Hindu*, August 29, 2004.

[23] An internal army enquiry admitted that there were "some lapses by the Assam Rifles personnel in implementation of instructions issued by army authorities for the conduct of search operations", but did not indicate what the lapses were. (*Tehelka*, August 7, 2004.)

[24] Khatoli Khala, *The Armed Forces (Special Powers) Act and Its Impact on Women in Nagaland* (New Delhi: WISCOMP Perspectives 5, 2003), pp. 26–27.

[25] Ibid.

[26] Anuradha M. Chenoy, "Implications of Insurgencies on Women: India", unpublished paper.

[27] Ibid.

[28] Ibid. See also *"Everyone Lives in Fear": Patterns of Impunity in Jammu & Kashmir*, Report of Human Rights Watch, September 2006, published after this monograph was written.

[29] Press Council of India, *Speaking Peace—a Report.*

[30] Khatoli Khala, op. cit., pp. 49–54.

[31] Ibid., pp. 55–57.

[32] As reported in *Tehelka*, August 7, 2004.

[33] Press Council of India, *Crisis and Credibility* (New Delhi: Lancer International, 1991), p. 127.

[34] As reported in *The Hindustan Times*, August 12, 2004.

[35] Anuradha M. Chenoy, op. cit.

[36] See Ritu Menon and Kamla Bhasin, *Borders & Boundaries: Women*

in India's Partition, op. cit., for various accounts of women's resistance and forms of protest in the face of extreme violation.

[37] See Veena Das, "Our Work to Cry, Your Work to Listen" in Das (ed.), *Mirrors of Violence: Communities, Riots and Survivors in South Asia* (New Delhi: Oxford University Press, 1990), p. 363.

[38] For a most illuminating discussion on the critical role played by memory in situations of state repression, see Elizabeth Jelin, op. cit.; and especially her analysis of gendered memory, pp. 76–89.

[39] The Displaced Persons (Claims) Act, 1950 (New Delhi: National Archives of India).

[40] For a fuller discussion of this aspect see Ritu Menon, "Birth of Social Security Committments: What Happened in the West", in Ranabir Samaddar (ed.), *Refugees and the State: Practices of Asylum and Care in India, 1947–2000* (New Delhi: Sage Publications, 2003).

[41] A detailed review of this Act and its repercussions is contained in Menon and Bhasin, *Borders & Boundaries*, op. cit.

[42] As maintained in conversation by an anonymous army source.

[43] Figures are based on information provided by a retired army general who wishes to remain anonymous.

[44] Press Council of India, *Crisis and Credibility*, op. cit., p. 113.

[45] Ibid., p. 235.

[46] Ibid., pp. 127, 130.

[47] Ibid., p. 215.

[48] Ibid., p. 215.

[49] Ibid., p. 217.

[50] Ibid., p. 102.

[51] Elizabeth Jelin, *State Repression*, op. cit., p. 76, discusses this contrast at length. Speaking of the Mothers of the Plaza de Mayo in Argentina and of the resistance to Pinochet in Chile, she says it was women who ran the human rights organizations, demanding justice; they were also the most visible presence in street demonstrations against the General. The same is true of Pakistan in our region, where the Women's Action Forum was the one collectivity that came out on the streets to protest General Zia ul Huq's Islamisation project and the infamous Hudood Ordinances.

[52] Ibid., p. 82.

[53] Ibid., p. 80.

[54] Tanika Sarkar, "Semiotics of Terror", op. cit., p. 2875.
[55] Siddharth Varadarajan (ed.), *Gujarat: The Making of Tragedy* (New Delhi: Penguin Books, 2002), p. 8.
[56] Wendy Brown, *States of Injury: Power and Freedom in Late Modernity*, op. cit., pp. 186–189.
[57] Upendra Baxi, "The Gujarat Catastrophe", op. cit., pp. 341–42. For its part, the NHRC was unequivocal in its indictment of state inaction. It stated clearly that it is the state's responsibility not only to protect the right to life, liberty and equality of its citizens, but also to prevent their violation through abetment, overt acts or negligence. It further noted a "serious failure of intelligence and action by the state government, leading to the Godhra incident and subsequent riots."

The tone and tenor of the NCW Report on Gujarat mark a significant departure from its response over the years to other major instances of violence against women. In the Bhanwari Devi rape case, for instance, its position and findings were contrary to those of the state enquiry commissions, as well as the Central Bureau of Investigation. Similarly, its investigations into the case of Lalitha Oraon's brutalization at the hands of an IFS officer in France ran counter to the official version, raising troubling questions about the latter's veracity.

Its Report on Gujarat, however, pointedly evades the issue of state and administrative culpability. Through a curious combination of staccato, deadpan prose ("Women have complained of extreme violence including some cases of sexual assault and rape. Many have lost their lives also. Several pathetic cries and pleas came before the Committee"), and pious sentiments ("Now is the time to look ahead rather than backwards. The administration, the community, NGOs and media need to forge partnerships to restore normalcy in the state of Gujarat;" and "To ensure that justice is done to women, government should perform its constitutional duty") it managed to deflect government accountability and, at the same time, position all the players—government, NGOs, victims, perpetrators and law enforcers—on the same plane, regardless of all acts of omission and commission on the part of the government.

The NCW Committee comprised members of the Commission, the Director General of the BSF, two Supreme Court advocates, and two respected and senior representatives of women's organizations. The presence of the last-mentioned both legitimized the Report and lent it poignancy, for the language of the Report, as well as its findings and recommendations, betray the kind of bureaucratese that neither condemns nor exonerates—it merely whitewashes.

[58] Wendy Brown, op. cit., p. 191.

mally [illegible] spotted the sensor representation [illegible] of women's organi-
zations. The presence of the [illegible] both legitimized the
Report and lent it perspective for the [illegible] of the Report, as
well as its findings and recognition [illegible] the kind
that [illegible] that need of confidentiality [illegible] and more
[illegible]

[38] Wendy Brown, op. cit., p. 191.